# The Supernatu

Peter Haining is a full-time writer whose books include *Elvis in Private, The Great English Earthquake* and *The English Highwayman*. Previously a journalist and a publisher, he brings to his work the resources of an extensive personal library of books and periodicals.

Peter Haining is married with three children and lives in Suffolk.

# The Supernatural Coast

*UNEXPLAINED MYSTERIES OF EAST ANGLIA*

Peter Haining

ROBERT HALE · LONDON

ISBN 0 7090 4722 3

Robert Hale Limited
Clerkenwell House
Clerkenwell Green
London EC1R 0HT

Photoset in North Wales by
Derek Doyle & Associates, Mold, Clwyd.
Printed in Great Britain by
St Edmundsbury Press Ltd, Bury St Edmunds, Suffolk.
Bound by Hunter & Foulis Ltd.

# Contents

You see, we believe in the supernatural in East Anglia
– or, if we do not admit that we believe in it, we have
a hair-raising collection of stories about it. And why
not? Is it not the old land of Thor and Odin, or Freya
and St. Guthlac, of Fenris the Wolf and St. Ingulph –
of old gods and old saints of Saxon and Dane, a land
of once-wild fens and steaming meres, of bare and
windy heaths and dark woods that run down to the
lonely, shining sea? Those old fens were a very
lurking place of demons and swart devils, of Will o'
the Wisp and Black Dogs. And still today there is a
North Sea magic in the night wind, the whisper of
witch-wings under the stars.

James Wentworth Day, 1954

For
MAC & JANET
– always raising a smile
on the coast!

# 1   A Night on the Supernatural Coast

It was one of those moonlit nights in early spring when every dark shape was turned into something sinister and every sound was magnified into a wail or a scream. A night when a town dweller like myself was glad to be in the company of a countryman born and bred who could differentiate between what was real and what was a trick of the light.

There were two of us out on the Essex marshes that night – oh, and a large, black dog that melted in and out of the shadows without a sound, his nostrils pricked for any unusual scent that floated by on the still night air. The North Sea, which was only a half a mile away from where we walked, was unusually calm, and there was not even the sound of water moving in the little creeks and rivers which meandered across the marshland.

We were on a ghost hunt, my companion and I, and as this area was one with which he was very familiar, he had chosen to bring me here to experience what the supernatural was really like far away from the city lights. Our destination was a wood on the edge of the marshes which was supposed to be haunted by the ghost of a Druid clothed in full regalia. This impressive figure had been seen several times in living memory by local people, my companion had told me, and always on the night of a full moon.

It was just such a night in April when the pair of us, clad in anoraks and thigh-length waders, trudged out beneath a glaring white moon to see what we might see in Druid's Wood ...

What was to prove an unforgettable night for me took place some years ago while I was writing a book about ghosts and hauntings. My late father-in-law, who was then the editor of the *Essex Weekly News* in Chelmsford, had suggested that I should talk to one of his contributors who, he said, was very knowledgeable about the supernatural in East Anglia. The man's name was James Wentworth Day, a former editor of *The Field*, a regular contributor to *Country Life*, and the author of several books featuring the supernatural.

Wentworth Day, who was the member of an East Anglian family who had owned landed property in the eastern counties for over 400 years, lived not far from the Essex coast in a town called Ingatestone. His home, close to the main railway line from Chelmsford to London, was appropriately just the kind of big, old house that looked as if it *should* be haunted.

My telephone call to him about my project was warmly received and ended with an invitation to meet him and accompany him to a spot on the coast which he said was haunted. I accepted gratefully ... but when, a few nights later, the pair of us were trudging across the desolate marshes, I had cause to wonder if it had been quite such a sensible decision after all.

The evening had begun with a lengthy discussion about the supernatural in the author's house. During the course of this chat he had recommended several books worthy of study as well as giving me a number of oral traditions to investigate. Then with a convivial tot of whisky to put us in the right spirits, we set off shortly after 11 p.m. for Tollesbury, a small village at the mouth of the River Blackwater close to where it joins the North Sea.

As we passed through Maldon, the last town of any size on our journey, James Wentworth Day told me he had spent many a day on the marshes hereabouts, either fishing or indulging in his other great passion for wild-fowling. He had come less frequently at night, he admitted, because of the tales he had been told of ghosts and witches and devils that haunted the area.

Wentworth Day was not a man who gave the impression of being easily scared. With his thin face and dark, brooding eyes behind round, steel-rimmed glasses, he seemed on first meeting a slightly menacing figure himself. Indeed, his renowned dislike for townies, whom he felt were hell-bent on urbanizing the countryside, made me a little uncertain of him to begin with. But once we had reached Tollesbury, abandoned the car, and set out onto the marshes with the dog at our heels, I felt I could not have had a better companion.

As we walked across the squelching earth, he told me that these marshes were among the loneliest on the east coast and had had a long association with the supernatural. Local people spoke of ghosts, devils, witches and wizards with a familiarity that made them sound like their neighbours. Which, in a way of course, they were.

The wood we were heading for gradually loomed up in front of us against the night sky as midnight neared. This place, my companion said, had a reputation for being devil ridden. Indeed, when some modern day Satanists came up from London and tried to hold one of their sex and black magic rituals in it, something far more terrifying than they had ever intended to raise appeared and so terrified them that they fled never to return. Local people had always maintained that the place had a reputation not to be treated lightly – as the Satanists had discovered at the cost of their sanity.

If I say my heart was beating faster as we walked into the wood, it would be an understatement. After only a few steps I imagined all sorts of stealthy movements and little sounds amongst the tall, dark trees and moved a bit closer to my guide.

Then, in an instant, the air was suddenly full of a devil's chorus of noise. Screeches such as one imagined only spirits of the dead might make shattered the stillness of the night. Instinctively, I looked upwards and half expected to see a flurry of ghostly figures passing overhead.

Instead, what I saw were slim, black figures, long and gaunt, darting among the treetops. They appeared to be between two to three feet high, with what seemed like cloaks flowing from them. The hair on the back of my neck rose and a shiver ran the length of my spine. Was I experiencing a genuine haunting? It certainly seemed so at that frozen moment of time.

The chorus of howls rose to a crescendo and I was conscious that the dog, just ahead of us, was now crouching on the ground with his hackles raised and growling deep in his throat. Only James Wentworth Day seemed to be unconcerned.

'My God,' I could only whisper as my heart threatened to burst out of my chest, 'what the devil is that row? And what on *earth* are those?'

The moonlight glinted on my companion's glasses as he turned around to face me. 'Scaring aren't they?' he asked. 'They frightened me, too, the first time I was brought to this wood.'

Above us the shapes were now thankfully disappearing among the trees, as he went on.

'An old herdsman – a "looker" as they call them around here – brought me out one night. We both had guns with us and when that caterwauling broke out I was so scared I raised my gun to fire. "Don't shoot," the old fellow told me. "You oughta know what they be, brought up on the marshes. Don't you know a gang of ole Frank Herons nesting when you see 'em?"

'I *should* have known,' Wentworth Day went on. 'But the moonlight, the shadows and the hideous cries the birds made as they took off just played on the superstitious side of my nature. I thought for a minute I was surrounded by some of the devil's own. I couldn't get out of the wood quickly enough after that. And I'm still not sure whether it was the ignominy of the situation or just plain fear that made me want to get back to the security of civilization as fast as I could.'

My own emotions were also so mixed at that moment that I knew precisely what he meant. After a few moments we went on further into the wood, but I somehow felt that we would see nothing further that night – and so it proved. Indeed, even if the Druid had chosen to haunt us I suspect it would have been an anticlimax after the hellish row of those birds.

Later, in the early hours of the morning when we were back in James Wentworth Day's book-lined study enjoying coffee and brandy, I silently writing up my last notes prior to putting away my notebook, my host spoke again.

'Of course, you might say that the "haunting" we experienced tonight had a rational explanation,' he said, 'but there are a lot of others on the East Anglian coast which you cannot explain away. Stories of strange creatures and strange events that no-one has an answer for.

'If you can get the trust of the people who have lived on the coast all their lives you'll get enough material not just for one book but for several. I've been traipsing about this part of England for years and I'm sure I've only scratched the surface. It's something to think about ...'

It certainly was. James Wentworth Day continued to 'traipse about' East Anglia until his death in 1983, and produced another excellent collection, Essex Ghosts, in 1973. His words also remained in the back of the mind of the person who had shared his experience on the Essex marshes that April night – me. So much so in fact, that they have led me to write this book both as a record of my discoveries during my own travels around the coastline of this part of England – where I too have now lived for a considerable part of my life – and as tribute to the memory of James Wentworth Day.

I did at one stage think of returning again to that haunted wood on the marshes to see if this time I could see the ghost of the Druid. But even knowing beforehand what caused that explosion of unearthly sounds, the thought of facing them without the companionship of my friend somehow deterred me. In truth, I prefer to leave the herons to their domain, and instead relate the other many strange and mysterious stories which I have discovered while exploring 'the supernatural coast' ...

The coastline of East Anglia is probably the most easily recognized on the entire map of the British Isles. A rounded shore thrusting into the North Sea rather like the chest of a pouter pigeon, it sweeps from The Wash to the Thames with scarcely a break anywhere to allow for a river or an estuary.

It is a coast not easy to circumnavigate by road, for such has been the pounding by the dark and remorseless North Sea over the centuries that any carriageways too close to the shore would long ago have been swept away. Indeed, I doubt if there is any other coastline in the British Isles which has been more changed by the sea or more constantly under its threat. The geography, history and social conditions of the East Anglian shore have all truly been shaped by this sea.

Although it has its occasional big towns and ports – Great Yarmouth, Lowestoft, Felixstowe, Harwich, Clacton and Southend-on-Sea – the coast of East Anglia is in the main a place of little fishing villages and small holiday resorts. Not forgetting the great expanses of marshland, the long, remote stretches of headland and miles of unspoiled, deserted beaches.

P.D.James, one of today's finest novelists, has long been attracted by the East Anglian coast and on occasions used it as the location for her compelling and ingenious murder stories. She believes that the setting in a work of fiction is very important, especially to a crime writer who deals in the abnormal, the horrific and the bizarre. For, as she says, it will help root the action in reality and enhance the suspense and terror of the drama as it unfolds. Nowhere strikes her as quite so suited to fulfil these needs than East Anglia, as she wrote in an essay for the *Observer* in January 1986:

> This coastal strip still seems one of the most remote parts of England. There are few main roads and fewer railways, no lure for the tourist bent on bright lights and raucous pleasures. It is a coast of marsh and heathland, of tracks almost as old as recorded time leading through thin woodlands to solitary shingled beaches, to dunes clumped

with shivering marram grass and delicately jewelled with
sea-holly, sandwort and sea-spurge.

This coast, in particular the stretch beween Lowestoft and
Southend, also has a special fascination for me, and over
the years I have found that there are few better places to
escape from the hustle and bustle of life than the small
resorts of Southwold, Aldeburgh, Walton-on-the-Naze or
Mersea. Each has retained its own character, be it
ever-so-slightly-grand or humbly basic, and allowed those
who live there to retain their own ways despite the influx
of tourists and weekenders. It is, indeed, from the
experiences of these local people that the stories in this
book have been mostly drawn.

They are, without exception, enduring stories. Tales of
strange supernatural encounters with the seen and the
unseen which have been reported over the years and
handed from parent to child, generation after generation,
without scepticism or ridicule. Modern science and
technology might wish to scoff at some of the legends, but
then it is easy to laugh in a safe environment with
electricity to see by and a fire to warm the chill night air.
But on the East Anglian coast when the night is starless,
when the sea is in turmoil and the wind is howling, try
and walk alone and not believe the footsteps behind might
be a giant hound or the shape ahead that of a ghost.
Nothing here is easy to dismiss as a mere figment of the
imagination.

But this is not, however, just a book about the
supernatural on land. The sea along this shore has also
thrown up its fair share of mysteries, and herein will be
found reports of mermaids, sea monsters and drowned
communities where church bells still ring. Sometimes the
land and sea even merge, for the supernatural knows no
boundaries and a phantom may just as easily walk on the
water as a sea spirit can come onto land.

Travelling along the East Anglian coast is rather like
entering a secret and occasionally eerie world. The endless
miles of heath and marshland are crossed by narrow roads
that bear all the signs of having changed little for

centuries. And all the time there are the grey and
enigmatic waters of the North Sea, which even on the
warmest summer day still seem to exude the chill of
fathomless depths.

At night particularly, it is easy to understand why
M.R.James, the famous ghost story writer, should have
found the inspiration for some of his best supernatural
stories from this coast. He, too, grew up in East Anglia and
experienced how the wind can often moan like a soul in
torment and twist the trees and foliage into the strangest
shapes. (*Vide* that classic short story *Oh, Whistle, and I'll
Come To You, My Lad*). The rich store of local ghost yarns
told with such relish and conviction can only have excited
his storyteller's imagination more.

I am dealing with facts here rather than fiction however.
And in this context I owe a debt of gratitude to those many
people around East Anglia who were prepared to share
with me their knowledge of their 'supernatural coast' –
passing on stories they had heard, and unearthing old
newspapers, documents and even family records to
support their accounts. It has been a pleasure to commit
their memories to paper to ensure they are on record for
posterity.

I shall, of course, be pleased to hear from anyone who
can add further information to any of the stories in this
book. For like all good real life mysteries, I am sure there is
more to discover that only time and further research will
reveal. Finally, may I urge the reader who has not done so
to visit the supernatural coast. For just as the great English
theologian, Cardinal John Henry Newman once wrote in
his *Grammar of Assent* (1870), 'He who has once seen a
ghost is never again as though he had not seen a ghost'.
No visitor to this shoreline of mysteries is ever quite the
same again ...

# 2    The Sirens of The Wash

Snettisham Beach which faces across the vast, flat vista of
The Wash is a long expanse of shingle and sand backed by
a high embankment. This man-made bulwark protects the
low-lying land behind from the tides as well as offering
birdwatchers an unparalleled assembly of wildlife to gaze
at. Indeed, it is claimed that the second largest
concentration of wading birds in Britain are to be found
hereabouts, a mixture of curlew, dunlin, redshank, knot
and oyster-catcher. Small wonder that the RSPB should
have established a reserve at the southern end of the
beach where four hides enable visitors to watch these
teeming varieties to their hearts' content.

The area has, in fact, a long-standing reputation for
attracting rare varieties of birds to complement the many
thousands of common terns who are so much in evidence
in the summer, and the waders and wildfowl in the
winter. Several writers have referred to the place as 'siren
haunted', and no present day visitor will take long to
discover why this stretch of coast should be one of the best
known in Britain for stories of those fabled sea creatures,
the sirens: perhaps better known as the seductive
mermaid.

It is easy, of course, to be scornful of tales about
creatures supposed to be half human and half fish. Easy,
that is, until the sceptic finds himself actually beside the
beguilingly flat and sandy reaches of The Wash where the
sky and sea seem often to merge into one. For this is a
deceptive landscape of shifting sands and insidious tides
which moves faster than a man can walk and has an

almost hallucinatory effect on the senses. On dazzling summer days for instance, mirages are commonplace with buildings, small boats and even human figures, all seeming to hover above the hazy landscape.

And it is this sense of illusion that the sceptic will seize upon in his explanation for the tales of mermaids. For isn't it true that hundreds of seals live here and there can be no denying that over the years many people have mistaken these mammals for the legendary sirens? But to the folk who live along the stretch of coast where Norfolk meets Lincolnshire there is no such easy dismissal of a tradition that has survived in both oral tales and written accounts for so long. A tradition that has been further comme-morated in the Snettisham village sign which depicts two sea creatures holding aloft a golden torque. (This torque was one of six found on a local estate belonging to Sir Stephen Lycett-Green in 1948.)

Despite the fact that the shape of The Wash has been much changed by land reclamation since the early part of the seventeenth century – and now gives the impression of being part of the North Sea on maps of England – it is in fact the estuary of several rivers draining from the middle of the country and contains hundreds of square miles of mud-flats. At low tide these flats are shared by lone fishermen – seeking to earn a living collecting oysters, cockles and bait for fishing – and the multitude of birds searching for crustaceans, insects and worms to sustain their own existences.

It is on the sand-banks further out in The Wash that the seals can be seen, whole herds of both the common and grey variety, living and breeding contentedly. But if these are the original 'mermaids', say the folk around Snettisham, why is there a stretch of mud-flat known as Mermaid Sand and why are there memorials of them around the coast and legends about them which date back hundreds of years?

I suppose that for many people The Wash has a strong association with royalty, and certainly this is what brings large numbers of them to the area. Treasure seekers, for example, are lured by stories of King John's treasure.

Indeed, a royal baggage train carrying coins and valuables which was lost in a quicksand not far from Walpole St.Andrew in 1216, lies hidden there to this day awaiting rediscovery. (According to local people the most likely location is somewhere beneath the 9-hole golf course at Sutton Bridge which was for centuries a tract of marshland!) For royal family watchers, there is the draw of Sandringham House, the 20,000 acre estate said to be the Queen's favourite holiday haunt where she entertains during the winter months. I use the word 'haunt' deliberately for its tale of ghosts and those of mermaids in the nearby Snettisham go hand-in-hand in local lore. (Sandringham is, incidentally, open to the public on most days from Easter until the end of September, with the exception of the last week of July and first week of August.)

The 274-roomed, mock-Jacobean style mansion was built by King Edward VII when he was Prince of Wales in 1870, and is today a mixture of the grand and the homely where the royal family can go shooting by day and entertain around roaring fires by night. The ghost of Sandringham is said to make his presence felt on Christmas Eve, creating the sound of hollow footsteps, moving objects about and switching lights on and off. It has been suggested that the ghost might be that of either King George V who died there in 1936 or George VI who also passed away at Sandringham in 1952, although both of these seem unlikely as the phantom had been reported in the Victorian era.

The first man to write about this haunting was the Reverend Gerard W.Bancks, the vicar of nearby Ingoldsthorpe, who several times conducted Christmas services for the Prince of Wales and other royals while they were staying at Sandringham. His interest in the supernatural extended beyond ghosts however, and there is evidence that he was intrigued by the local legends of mermaids. In 1890 he published a curious and undoubtedly much fictionalized work entitled *A World Beneath The Waters*, in which he endeavoured to make a case for there being an underwater colony off the East Anglian coast.

What, though, makes the Reverend Bancks's book particularly interesting is that it tells the story of two children who saw a mermaid on Snettisham beach. And although the author undoubtedly embellished the facts to add verisimilitude to his theory, the story is substantially true according to several of the older residents of the village. According to them, the story was based on the eye-witness account of a brother and sister who were well-known in the district and Reverend Bancks's version of their story reads as follows:

> The two children, a boy and girl, were quite used to wander along the coast by themselves, even at night. They had been this evening to carry fishing lines down to their father's boat, and were on the way home when an object in the sea attracted their attention. They had not been watching for more than a few moments before something very extraordinary happened. When the object had rolled into shallow water, it suddenly slid onto some low rocks a short distance from the shore. There it threw off from around it a loose garment and sat down. The moon was shining so brightly that the children could see quite distinctly.
>
> 'Why, it's a girl,' cried the boy, and sure enough it was – a pretty little girl with long dark hair that hung half-way down her back. And presently she began to sing in a sweet, low voice.
>
> The children watched her with equal interest and astonishment, but so anxious were they to hear what it was she was singing, and to observe her every movement, that they were not sufficiently careful to keep themselves hidden. The little stranger evidently caught a glimpse of them, for she hurriedly rose, wrapped the garment around her, and in a very few moments had dived into the sea. Spellbound, the children watched to see her rise to the surface, but she appeared no more.
>
> 'She can't be like other children, Tony,' said the girl at last, 'or she would be drowned. Do you think she can be one of the mermaids that father says live in the sea?'
>
> 'Maybe,' said Tony, 'for in that cloak of hers folks would hardly know whether she were girl or fish.'

In a later chapter of Reverend Bancks's story, the children meet the mermaid again and are taken by her to visit the 'world beneath the waves' – but no such claim was ever made by the brother and sister from Snettisham, according to the information I was given.

This legend also came to the attention of Henry Williamson, the author of those two classic nature stories, *Tarka the Otter* (1927) and *Salar the Salmon* (1935), who lived in Norfolk for many years. Commenting on the tradition in Norfolk in an essay for the *Eastern Daily Press* in 1943, he began by agreeing with a seventeenth century writer on mermaids that, 'It is no fabulous tale that is told of them,' and continued:

A friend told me that in the Middle Ages mermaids were held to be the souls of the damned, ex-communicated from the sacraments of the Mother Church, so they came up from the sea and pressed themselves against the North Door to catch an echo of the Holy Mass from which they were shut out. This, she said, is the explanation of the mermaids portrayed on North doors and poppy heads on North aisles, so I was most interested to find one in Cley Church.

But why the north? Mermaids, it was believed, took human form at will, and sometimes married mortals, but those drawn by the sea-woman's strange, cold eyes, were sucked into 'unseen whirlpools', and were damned also for having sought a joy and beauty beyond what this old green earth can give. Sooner or later the sea-wife went back to the sea leaving them to wander on life's path alone.

Cley Church, which Henry Williamson refers to, is not far from Snettisham – situated in a small seaside community between the towns of Hunstanton and Sheringham – and the mention of the mermaid carving there is another indication of the association these sirens have with the East Anglian coast – a fact which research soon substantiates....

There is a comprehensive definition of the mermaid to be found in the excellent *Funk & Wagnalls Dictionary of Folklore, Mythology and Legend* (1975) which is worth noting before looking at specific examples. The entry reads as follows:

*Mermaid.* A supernatural sea-dwelling female of general European maritime folklore. They are usually depicted as having the head and body of a woman to the waist, and a tapering fish body and tail instead of legs. They live in an undersea world of splendour and riches, but have been known to assume human form and come ashore to markets and fairs. These beautiful, sirenlike women often lure mariners to their destruction, and are said to gather the souls of the drowned and cage them in their domain. It is generally thought unlucky to see a mermaid; the sight of one presages storm or disaster, and they often lead people astray. Getting hold of any garment of a mermaid gives one power over her. The marriage of a mortal man to a mermaid is common in folktale and folk belief; descendants of such a union are said to be still living in Machaire, Ireland.

Although there are no such stories of the offspring of mermaids to be found in East Anglia, the tradition is nevertheless deeply entrenched in local legend, and stories can be heard all along the coast from The Wash to Yarmouth and The Broads. Physical evidence can also be seen in the number of carved mermaids to be found adorning churches such as the little siren who gazes seawards from the end of a pew in the nave of All Saints' at Upper Sheringham on the Norfolk coast. Other similar examples are on view at Ufford, Freckenham, Lakenheath, Stowlangtoft, Withersfield and Blytheburgh. The little mermaid in this last church is perhaps the most beautiful of them all and is located on a pew just behind the south porch door where she rests beguilingly on her tail, which stretches out horizontally from her torso.

Also, in a number of the small fishing villages it is quite possible to find old salts who will recount stories of these famous sea dwellers – which they tell with a mixture of scepticism and a healthy respect for the beliefs of their forebears. Indeed, once their accounts are amalgamated with the reference to mermaids in a number of books and local newspaper reports, the area can be seen to possess a rich and fascinating mermaid history.

It seems clear that the earliest stories of mermaids

predate biblical times, but have actually changed very little in character over the centuries. The creatures are said to resemble beautiful girls with the exception of having fish tails where there should be legs. They are invariably naked, though some possess long hair which may be modestly draped over their breasts. All mermaids are said to be seen sitting on a rock or sand-bank combing their long tresses and singing with voices of irresistible sweetness. It is the combination of their voices and their beauty which legend says has lured many a sailor to his fate.

Curiously, although in many other parts of Europe and Scandinavia the mermaid is said to be an omen of storms and disasters who will quite shamelessly lure sailors to their death, in East Anglia the creature is seen in a much more romantic light. Since the thirteenth century, reports indicate that people have viewed her as rather waif-like, seeking only to attract a human mate to share her lonely life beneath the waves.

The Roman historian Pliny was one of the first to write about these creatures in the seas around Britain, declaring in his *Historia Naturalis* (AD 77), 'The Ambassadors to Augustus from Gaul declared that sea-women were often seen in their neighbourhood.' His report was also substantiated by two other Roman writers, Solinus and Aulus Gellius, citing accounts from countrymen who had visited East Anglia.

Further early references are to be found in the *Histoire d'Angleterre* written in the twelfth century in which it is stated:

> Amongst the sea monsters which are in the North Sea and are often seen, first place must be given to the mermaid. The existence of this creature is questioned by many, nor is it to be wondered at, because most of the accounts we have had of it are mixed with mere fables and may be looked upon as idle tales. But whilst we have no grounds to believe all these fables, yet as to the existence of the creature we may safely give our assent to.

Among the reports this work lists as being reliable is one t on of a mermaid seen off the coast of Norfolk in the twelfth century. The creature had very white skin, black hair hanging down her back and 'the tail of a porpoise speckled like that of a mackerel.'

If the people of Norfolk felt any fear of being laughed at for telling such a story, they need not have worried, for some other even more remarkable encounters were to follow. In 1430, for example, just across the other side of the North Sea in Holland, a mermaid was actually taken alive. The best account of this event is to be found in the pages of the *Norfolk News* – another indication of local interest in the subject – in a column entitled 'Curiosities and Wonder' published in 1714. The story is headlined MERMAID FOUND IN HOLLAND and reads:

> In 1430, after a violent tempest which had broken down the dikes of Holland, some milkmaids of Edam, a town upon Zuyder-Zee, going in a boat from thence to Promerand, found a mermaid left in the mud with very little water. They took her into their boat, washed her clean, and brought her to Edam, where they dressed her in woman's apparel, taught her to spin, and fed her the same as themselves. Sometime afterwards, she was sent to Haarlem, where she lived several years; but could not be brought to speak, or even attempt it, and always showed an inclination to return to the water. They taught her to make the sign of the cross, and to pay a sort of reverence to a crucifix, and on her death she was allowed a Christian burial.

What may well have prompted the *Norfolk News* to carry the story was the fact that in that same year of 1714, a Dutch geographer and travel writer named Francois Valentijn reported seeing a mermaid while sailing from Batavia to Europe. The creature, he said, in his *Travels* (1714), 'was sitting on the surface of the water, with its back towards me; the body was half above water and was of a grizzly colour, like that of a cod-fish; it had breasts and was shaped like a woman above the waist, and from thence downwards went tapering off to a point.'

Another interesting eighteenth century French report

quoted by Osbert Sitwell in *Sober Truth* (1930) describes a mermaid rather different from her sisters in that her lower body was divided into two tapering tails, 'looking for all the world like two legs covered in scales'. This particular sighting has been commemorated by a carving in the Puce Church in Gironde, which can still be seen today.

There was still more public excitement and interest in the year 1794 when an East Anglian fisherman named Captain Fortier sailed out of Yarmouth and was said to have captured a mermaid in the North Sea. According to reports the captain later sold his prize for a considerable sum to a London showman who promptly began to exhibit it in Covent Garden. An account of the show published in the *London Gazette* that same year declared. 'This nymph of the sea, a woman from the head down to the lower part of the waist, and a fish from thence downwards, was three feet long, having ears, gills, breasts, fins, shoulders, arms, hands, fingers and a contiguous scale covering the fish part.'

Unfortunately, though the *Gazette* is fulsome in its details about the hordes of curiosity seekers who paid their admission fees to see the exhibit at 7, Broad Court, there is no further information about the mysterious Captain Fortier who landed this prize and I have been unable to trace any more details about him in Yarmouth.

There is also very little information about an East Anglian-born mariner named John Robinson who is said to have been actually saved from drowning by a mermaid at the close of the eighteenth century. His amazing story is recorded in a rare pamphlet entitled – with good reason! – *The Wonder of Wonders*, a copy of which is possessed by the British Museum. The pamphlet is illustrated with a curious wood engraving of a two-tailed mermaid and subitled, 'A Strange and Wonderful Relation of a Mermaid that was seen and spoke with, on the Black Rock nigh Liverpool, by John Robinson, mariner, who was tossed on the Ocean for Six days and Nights; Together with the Conversation he had with her, and how he was preserved; with the Manner of his Death five days after his return Home.'

At first glance the pamphlet could easily be dismissed as a typical catchpenny piece of fiction foisted on a public that enjoyed sensation. But thanks to some diligent research by the British Museum, the pamphlet is annotated with the fact that John Robinson died at Old Hunstanton, not far from the famous town of Hunstanton on The Wash, in May 1798. So although what follows may well be a highly coloured account of a very traumatic experience at sea, the subject of the report did actually exist.

According to this pamphlet, on 29 April 1798, a ship, the *Dolphin*, was sailing from Amsterdam to Liverpool only to be battered by a terrible storm which killed all the crew but one – young John Robinson who had been lying ill in his bunk below deck. When he awoke, says the account, he found himself alone 'left to Almighty Providence and to the Mercy of the Seas and Winds, and he was in great Fear and dreadful Fright on the Main Ocean.' The publication continues:

But to his great Amazement, he espy'd a beautiful young Lady combing her hair, and toss'd on the Billows, cloathed all in green (but by chance he got the first word with her) then she with a Smile came on board and asked how he did. The young Man being Something Smart and a Scholar, reply'd, 'Madam I am the better to see you in good Health, in great hopes trusting you will be a comfort and assistance to me in this my low Condition'; and so caught hold of her Comb and Green Girdle that was about her Waist. To which she replied 'Sir, you ought not to rob a young Woman of her Riches, and then expect a favour at her Hands; but if you will give me my Comb and Girdle again, what lies in my powers, I will do for you.'

At which Time he had no Power to keep them from her, but immediately delivered them up again; she then smiling, thank'd him, and told him, If he would meet her again next Friday she would set him on shore. He had no power to deny her, so readily gave his Consent; at which time she gave him a Compass and desired him to steer South West: he thank'd her and told her he wanted some News. She said she would tell him the next opportunity when he fulfilled his promises; but that he would find his Father and Mother much grieved about him, and so jumping into the Sea she departed out of his sight.

At her departure the Tempest ceased and blew a fair Gale to South West, so he got safe on shore; but when he came to his Father's House he found every thing as she had told him. He was still very much troubled in his mind concerning his promise, but yet while he was thus musing, she appeared to him with a smiling Countenance and (by his Misfortune) she got the first word to him, so that he could not speak one Word, but was quite Dumb, yet he took Notice of the Words she spoke; and she began to Sing. After which she departed out of the young Man's sight, taking from him the Compass.

She took the Ring from off her Finger and put it on the young Man's and said she expected to see him once again with more Freedom. But he never saw her more, upon which he came to himself again, went home, and was taken ill, and died in five days after, to the wonderful admiration of all the people who saw the young man.

It might well be argued that this whole story should be read as a case of delusion brought upon young John Robinson by the terrible trauma of the storm that nearly drowned him. Certainly the tale is full of improbabilities, but none the less deserves a place in the legend of the mermaid as an example of a deal being struck between a member of the human race and a sea dweller.

There is one further story relating to East Anglia from the nineteenth century which should be included before we reach the era of living memory. This is taken from the files of the *Lincolnshire Chronicle* and concerns a mermaid apparently taken captive by six fen men in the summer of 1832.

There has appeared in the London press a curious communication on the subject of mermaids from a Mr Lawrence Edmondstone of King's Lynn. He says that an animal answering to the following description, so far as the account of the six fishermen who captured it can be depended upon, was actually in their possession for three hours, but unluckily from some superstitious dread of injuring it, they returned it to its native element, and thus prevented the scientific identification of an animal which appears to have resembled what has generally been regarded as a merely fabulous creation.

Length of the creature, three feet; body without scales or hair; silver grey above, whitish below like the human skin; no gills were observed, no fins on the back or belly; tail like that of a dog fish; body very thick over the breast; by the eye the girth might be between two and three feet; the short neck, very distinct from the head and shoulders; the body rather depressed; the anterior extremities like the human hand, about the length of a seal's paw, webbed to about an inch of the ends of the fingers; mammae as large as those of a woman; mouth and lips very distinct and resembling the human.

Sceptics of the time were apparently soon responding to this report stating that there was a perfectly simple explanation to what the six fen men had caught. It was not a mermaid at all, but a manatee or dugong, a warm-blooded sea mammal. The Norfolk men had simply been unable to tell the difference beween a sea-cow and a fish-woman, these 'experts' insisted. The fen mens' reply was brief and to the point – manatees and dugongs only inhabit tropical coasts, any fool knows that!

Explanations such as this have, in fact, continued to be advanced in the twentieth century by 'experts' whenever sightings of mermaids have been reported. But, as the folk around the East Anglian coast will insist, these people can say what they like because the mermaid tradition cannot be so easily explained. And there are also some scientists who are having second thoughts too, as I shall explain.

Today, evidence of the allure of the mermaid can be found at a number of East Anglian coastal resorts. Beautiful drawings of them have been used in promotional booklets and advertisements, while there is hardly an important seaside festival in the region which does not feature some young lady in a fish tail as one of its main attractions!

There are also two intriguing modern stories of mermaids to add, by a pair of men with a lifetime of knowledge of East Anglian traditions. And it is true to say that neither James Wentworth Day nor Sidney Grapes were men easily fooled or deluded.

Sidney Grapes, a radio broadcaster and a member of the famous Grapes family of Potter in East Norfolk, delighted in telling the story of the day a fisherman from Winterton Ness caught a mermaid. There are those who claim the story he told on the radio is apocryphal; Sidney believed there to be an element of truth in it.

This old fellow and his son were fishing one day off Winterton Ness when they suddenly pulled a mermaid out of the sea in their net. The old man took the pretty little thing out of the net and turned it over with his hands several times. Finally he took a long squint at the catch, spat over the side of the boat, and then threw the creature back into the water again. The young man looked at him in amazement. 'Why?' he said. To which the old man replied with a suggestive grunt, 'How?'

James Wentworth Day, the author of numerous books on East Anglia, and an excellent fisherman and shot, has provided a rather more detailed account of a mermaid on the Norfolk coast, though he does not give a precise location. He recounted the events in a radio broadcast in 1954.

A farmer whose house was close to the coast was about to descend onto the shore one summer morning in 1926 when he saw a woman washing herself in the sea. At least he thought it was a woman and was about to turn back to spare her modesty when he had a second thought. Surely a woman would not go that far out into the sea, especially as the tide was high and he was certain the water was at least six foot where she was standing. After considering the matter, the farmer threw himself down on his face and crept to the edge of the rocks from which he had a good view of the woman for more than half an hour. At the end of this careful scrutiny, he crept back to call his family to see the wonderful sight. The family were all a little sceptical of his story, but dutifully followed him back to the seashore. When the man's wife arrived, however, she did not throw herself down as the others had done, but walked on until she was in sight of the creature. At this the mermaid – for that was what the creature surely was – dived into the water and swam away until she was a safe distance from the family. As she swam the whole family ran along the shore for more than half a mile during which time the mermaid's head and shoulders were visible in the water.

Recalling the event afterwards, the family said that there was a large stone, more than a yard in height, in the sea, on which the mermaid stood when she was first seen. She was standing out of the water from her waist up, and the whole family declared that she was exactly the same as a young woman of about eighteen years of age, both in shape and stature. Her hair was short, and of a dark colour; her face handsome, her neck and arms were like those of any ordinary woman, her breasts firm and her skin whiter than any person they had seen before. Her face was towards the shore. She bent herself down frequently, as if taking up water, and then holding her hand before her face for about half a minute. When she was thus bending herself, there was to be seen some black thing as if there was a tail turning up behind her. She often made some noise like sneezing, which caused the rock to echo. The farmer said afterwards that he had never seen a woman so handsome in appearance as this mermaid.

Michael Meurger, a Frenchman who lives in Paris and is probably today's leading researcher into mermaids, is equally convinced that accounts like these should be taken seriously.

'We must not assume that belief in such stories has faded simply because they are not reported,' he said recently. 'I have heard that mermaid stories are still transmitted in some conservative circles in Brittany, but discreetly. And I had a similar impression when I visited Norway in 1987, and yet what gets reported is generally some pressman's bunk such as the Lofoten Mermaid which was a pure hoax.'

Mr Meurger's quest for modern mermaid stories has brought him several convincing items from Britain including the sighting made in 1947 by an 80-year-old fisherman from the Isle of Muck, Inverness-shire who claimed he had seen one near the shore combing her hair. At Sandwood in Sutherland, which is traditionally called 'The Land of Mermaids', the appearance of sirens has been reported on several occasions during this century. And from Sutherland, too, there is a belief that members of the local Clan McVeagh are the descendants of a union between a mermaid and a fisherman.

Cornwall similarly has a strong mermaid tradition, the 'Mermaid's Rock' near Lamorna, which derived its name from a legendary creature who once haunted the spot and whose singing foretold shipwrecks, perhaps being the most famous. At Padstow there is also Doom Bar, a sand-bank which has caused many shipwrecks, and was reputedly created by a mermaid after a local resident fired a shot at her while she was bathing.

Interestingly, the songs of these sirens have from time to time been investigated by academics, including Professor John Chadwick of Downing College, Cambridge. He said a few years ago that although there is not enough authentic evidence to decipher what the language or purpose of the songs might be, there could be clues in a script allegedly written in Minoan Crete 4,000 years ago known as Linear A. Unfortunately, it has been impossible to translate more than a handful of the inscriptions on the fragmentary and incomplete document.

As I neared the end of my research into the mermaid tradition in East Anglia, there appeared yet another 'explanation' of their existence from a source on the other side of the Atlantic. According to two Canadian researchers, Dr W.H.Lehn, and Dr I.Schroeder, the sightings of these creatures could have been caused by optical distortion resulting from a particular set of weather conditions. Using the technology of a computer, the two men claimed that the tip of a whale or a walrus could assume the proportions of a mermaid when distorted by quirks of the atmosphere.

A report of their findings in *Nature* magazine said:

Experimenting on a computer with various values for the

temperatures of the air and sea, the height of the observer's eye above the water and his distance from the object, they were able to identify precise conditions in which a whale or a walrus just visible above the surface would appear in the form of a mermaid. They were able to confirm their conclusions on a spring morning on Lake Winnipeg. In atmospheric conditions such as they had defined, they photographed an apparent mermaid. It was, in fact, a boulder.

Such an explanation carried little weight among the people of The Wash with whom I discussed it. They knew all about the tricks of light from living on the edge of the hallucinatory water of that great estuary. And were they now to believe that all their ancestors had ever seen were a few rocks and suchlike sticking up out of the tide? No, sir!

If mermaids are less seen today, I heard it said, then it is because mankind is polluting the seas around our coast and driving these creatures to the more remote oceans of the world. And when they do come ashore – like the little mermaid in the Reverend Bancks's story – they cast off their fish skins and assume human form, looking no different to any other bather on the seashore.

'We're all drawn to the sea, aren't we?' one old East Anglian put it to me. 'Kind of irresistible isn't it, the way people always flock to the seaside? As if they have a basic need to be there. And don't they say that we evolved from the sea back in prehistoric times? Well, why shouldn't some of our kind, half fish and half man, still be out there? I reckon *that's* the explanation of your mermaid.'

I felt, then, there was nothing more I could add to my enquiries into the sirens of The Wash....

# 3　The Hell Hound of Cromer

The sun was just disappearing over the horizon leaving a shimmering, golden trail across the waves of the sea which was beginning to darken with the coming of evening. A large black dog came into view, pounding along the beach. It was difficult to tell from a distance the animal's breed, but as it passed by, its long strides keeping it just out of the waves hissing up onto the shingle, it looked very like a black labrador.

While I stood on the top of the cliffs watching the dog as it continued its powerful run in the direction of the setting sun, I felt a strange chill despite the air being far from cold. The animal's head was turned away and only a great red tongue was just visible hanging from one side of its massive jaws. Yet there was something eerie about the relentless pace it kept up and the ease with which it cleared one groyne after another, almost as if they were not there.

Behind me, as I stood lost in thought, the town of Cromer – the 'Gem of the Norfolk Coast' as it is called – was coming alive with lights and the bustle of holidaymakers. But somehow I was unable to take my eyes off the dog as it ran on, its shadow as black as the animal itself and lengthening with every stride it took up the shore in the direction of Sheringham.

A minute more and it was lost from sight. Almost reluctantly I turned to gaze back the way it had come – but there was no sign of the owner I expected to see following in the dog's wake. Indeed, the entire beach was deserted for as far as the eye could see.

An actual shiver ran up my spine then, and I felt the sight of the animal had been a kind of omen. For I had come to Cromer to investigate the legend of 'Black Shuck', the famous ghostly dog sometimes called 'Old Shuck' or even 'The Hell Hound'. This dog is said to have haunted the Norfolk coast for centuries and, close on one hundred years ago most probably played a part in inspiring one of the most famous of all the Sherlock Holmes stories, *The Hound of the Baskervilles*.

Let me say at once that I do *not* believe that I actually saw 'Black Shuck' late on that Sunday afternoon, but there was still something curious about the dog's solitary race along the beach when thought about in conjunction with the old legend and the Holmes story. For I knew the dog had been reported several times running along this particular beach from the vicinity of Overstrand towards East Runton Gap, and it had been on just such a Sunday back in 1905 that Sir Arthur Conan Doyle, the creator of the world's most famous detective, had heard all about 'Hell Hounds' while he was on holiday in the resort. I have to admit, too, that as I turned away from the sea and walked back into the town, I couldn't help feeling that the sighting had already added a little frisson of real life excitement to my research....

Behind the modern face that Cromer presents to its thousands of visitors each year lies a long and intriguing history. Indeed, according to Egon Jameson in *One Thousand Curiosities of Britain* (1947) it may well have been the home of the very first Briton. He writes:

'The earliest recorded inhabitant of Britain was called Eolithicus and he lived 500,000 years ago – that is some 6,666 generations back – and his dwelling place was in the hills near Cromer, Norfolk.'

To geologists however, Cromer means the Forest Bed, an estuarine deposit, almost certainly of the Rhine, which is exposed to the west and east of Cromer after unusually high tides have scoured the foot of the cliffs. Over the years a variety of animal fossils have been found hereabouts, some of the glacial period and some of the warmer interglacial period.

What is even more fascinating about the town is that it actually once stood someway inland behind a coastal town called Shipden-juxta-Mare which disappeared under the encroaching sea at the start of the fifteenth century. The town, according to various records, was 'a great and populous place, filled with thriving and opulent merchants,' and doubtless was a magnet for traders in much the same way as Dunwich, another 'lost town' on the East Anglian coast, which will feature in a later chapter.

A Victorian historian, Walter Rye, writing in his volume *Old East Anglia* at the turn of the century, summarized the events which occurred on this stretch of coast in these words:

> The place was certainly a trading port of some importance in the middle of the 14th Century, and it seems to have occupied low ground that has been submerged rather than high ground that the sea has washed away; for in a 17th Century record 'marshes' are mentioned which must have extended seaward of the cliffs and the names of 'Shippedenmere' and 'Chippedenmere', occurring in documents dated 1324 and 1326, suggest that the harbour may have been connected or identical with a marshland mere.
>
> Cromer iself was originally a hamlet of Shipden, situated, in all probability, at the seaward end of a valley opening out into the marshland; and as Shipden disappeared, house by house, and field by field, just as some of the coast villages are doing today, the hamlet increased in importance in consequence of Shipden's decay.

According to Mr Rye, the ruins of ancient Shipden's church, St Peter's, are said to be sometimes visible when the tide is unusually low – about 400 yards from the Cromer shore in the shape of a mass of squared flints. Not surprisingly this mound is referred to locally as the 'Church Rock'.

From early in the sixteenth century, Cromer apparently carried out a great deal of trade via the sea – in particular with Iceland and Norway – but further erosion of the cliffs and harbour brought about another change in its character so that it became a fishing village. By 1836, the quaint old houses and primitive jetty of the town caused it to be regarded as something of a 'fashionable bathing place' according to *White's Directory*. After this, and thanks to the careful planning of the Cabell family of Cromer Hall, the pleasing and individualistic Cromer of today emerged complete with its mixture of fishermen's cottages and houses for summer visitors. The Cabell family owned much of the land and only released plots for development on the understanding that the buildings would be in keeping with the neighbourhood.

There are a number of landmarks in Cromer which the local authority like to boast about as well as the area's long sandy beach and plentiful leisure activities. The magnificent church of St Peter & St Paul, which has a perpendicular tower over 160ft high and is the tallest in Norfolk, and the pier with its famous Pavilion Theatre offering genuine 'end of the pier entertainment' are two. Also, of course, there is the 58ft high lighthouse on cliffs 250ft high to the east of the town (the loftiest point on the Norfolk coast) which was built in 1833 and has a light that can be seen for 23 miles.

Local folk, however, prefer to talk about the delicious taste of their famous crabs and the skill of their lifeboatmen. In the Second World War, for instance, the Cromer lifeboat crew saved 450 lives and there is a bronze bust of the most famous coxswain, Henry Blogg, to be seen in North Lodge Park. And on any day, visitors will find the local fishermen's boats drawn up on the shore where their owners are selling the Cromer crab they have plucked fresh from the sea only hours before. In fact, when I was last in the town in April 1991, the talk was all about the landing of a rare blue crab – said to be one in ten million – which had just been caught by a local crabber, Billy Davis. This 'once in a blue moon' specimen was not destined for the table, however, but a local museum.

Up on the cliffs high above the town stands the Royal Cromer Golf Club, with an 18-hole course that draws players from far and wide, not just because of its excellent fairways and greens but also because it offers panoramic sea views. It was to the golf club that my research first took me because this was the place that had drawn Conan Doyle to the town for a holiday in 1905. Thus started the chain of events which culminated in the creation of his novel about the huge ghostly hound which brings such terror to the Baskerville family until the intervention of Sherlock Holmes.

Conan Doyle actually stayed at the Royal Links Hotel in Cromer for his golfing holiday, accompanied by a friend named Fletcher Robinson. Robinson was a tall, ebullient man from Newton Abbot who had apparently studied law but abandoned this profession in favour of journalism. His column in the *Daily Express* had made him a household name and it was at a literary soirée in London in the 1890's that he first met Conan Doyle and the two men became instant friends. Both shared an interest in tales of mystery (not forgetting golf!) and it therefore comes as no particular surprise to learn that while the two men were relaxing at Cromer 'one raw Sunday afternoon when a wind rushed off the North Sea' to quote Conan Doyle's own words, Robinson began telling him stories about spectral dogs.

There is, unfortunately, no precise information as to *why* this subject should have arisen – though there are three interesting explanations. The first is a local story. It is said that a chance remark by one of the waiters working in the Royal Links Hotel, commenting that it was on such days that 'Black Shuck' was known to run by on the beach, prompted the two visitors to begin a conversation on the topic. According to this version, the waiter's father had actually seen the dog running along the sands, and he knew that it was the creature of legend because it had huge, flaming red eyes. Conan Doyle would have found this tale particularly interesting because he was fascinated by the supernatural and a profound believer in ghosts.

A second suggestion is that either Conan Doyle or Fletcher Robinson may have glanced at a local guidebook, *The Norfolk Coast*, just issued that year by the *Norfolk News* Ltd of Norwich – a copy of which would certainly have been available for guests at the Royal Links Hotel. In the book was the following intriguing entry:

> Old Shuck is the grimmest apparition of the Norfolk coast. He takes the form of a huge black dog with a single flashing eye and a mouth that breathes forth fire, and to encounter him is an omen of dread significance: it means that you will die before the year is out. It is, perhaps, the oldest phantom in England; it has haunted our lonely roads for centuries. Probably it is of Norse origin – the Black Hound of Odin – and came to this coast with the Scandinavian raiders. Its lair is some secret place known only to itself, but some of its favourite haunts are known, and not many years ago there were men and women whom nothing would induce to venture into them after nightfall. When the wind howled around their isolated homes, it was the baying of Old Shuck they heard, and they trembled in their beds.
>
> There is a tale told along the coast of a practical joke played upon some fishermen by an auctioneer at Cromer, now dead. Knowing that the fishermen would be leaving a house about ten o'clock at night – the hour suggests the kind of house – the joker captured a black ram, wreathed it round with clanking chain, and kept it concealed behind a bank until the men came along the road. Just as they were passing the hiding-place, the ram was pushed down the steep bank right into the midst of them. The result of this dramatic appearance of 'Old Shuck' was a most disgraceful flight and no fishing for days!

It would not be giving away too much of the plot of Conan Doyle's famous Sherlock Holmes novel to point out that the hound in the story also, ultimately, proves to be a fraud.

A third version of the inspiration for the story says that it was Fletcher Robinson who first raised the subject while talking about his home on the borders of Dartmoor where there was a similar legend about a Hell Hound. Quite why he should have raised such an unlikely tale without some form of prompt is not easy to explain, but there is no doubt that Conan Doyle listened to his friend's account with avid interest *whatever* had sparked it off. Indeed, he was a man always on the lookout for new ideas for his work. Another interesting fact about which there is no dispute whatsoever is that the name of the Robinson family coachman at Newton Abbot was Harry Baskerville...

For the rest of their stay in Cromer the two friends played a round or two of golf each day, took long walks along the coastal path in both the Sheringham and Mundesley directions, and enjoyed the fine cuisine of the Royal Links which, sadly, later burned to the ground. Both men returned revitalized to London: Fletcher Robinson to take up a new appointment as editor of *Vanity Fair* magazine, and Conan Doyle's imagination so full of the story of the Hell Hound that it became one of only four full-length novels he wrote about his great detective.

When *The Hound of the Baskervilles* was published the following year, Conan Doyle gratefully acknowledged the sojourn in Cromer and the help of his friend in a dedication which read, 'This story owes its inception to my friend, Mr Fletcher Robinson, who has helped me both in the general plot and in the local details.'

Today, this Holmes adventure is regarded by many experts as the best of those four novels and perhaps even the very best of all the detective's cases. What also makes it unique in the Sherlockian canon is that it is the only tale in which the story dominates Holmes rather than Holmes dominating the story, as is the case in all the other adventures.

Certainly I would advise anyone who goes searching for 'Black Shuck' in Norfolk to first read *The Hound of the Baskervilles*, for it is infused with all the elements of mystery and terror which surround the real life legend of the spectral hound. It can also serve as a warning as to just what the unwary investigator might find himself confronted with! Interestingly, too, this is not the only Sherlock Holmes adventure which owes is origins to Norfolk. The highly regarded short story, *The Adventure of the Dancing Men* was also inspired by a visit Conan Doyle made to the village of Happisburgh some twelve miles down the coast. Firstly, however, there is more factual information that must be included about the legend of this terrifying supernatural dog in East Anglia.

As the Norfolk coast guidebook mentioned earlier says, 'Black Shuck' is believed to be one of the longest reported phantoms in English history, and certainly one of the best known in Norfolk where he has been spoken of for at least a thousand years. Most accounts also agree that the animal derived from that mighty dog of war, the Hound of Odin, which came to East Anglia when the Vikings first stormed these inlands; though the name itself perhaps offers the best clue for the term 'Shuck', coming from the Anglo-Saxon 'Scucca' or 'Sceocca', which is said to mean Satan or demon.

Several authorities say that the jet-black creature may appear as big as a fair sized calf, and has the ability to alter his appearance at will. It is the hound's usual practice to silently track lonely wayfarers, and he can terrify anyone with a single glance of his luminous eyes. Some reports indicate that the dog has occasionally been seen headless, while many folk claim that to meet 'Black Shuck' signifies death – or at the very least madness – within a year of the encounter.

What seems beyond doubt is that over the centuries there have been quite a number of sightings of the dog throughout East Anglia – as well as in certain other parts of southern England – but unlike the normal household pet he is more attached to places than people. The most consistent reports state that he is a shaggy-looking creature, easily distinguishable from ordinary dogs by his saucer sized eyes which flame with red fire. He tends to only emerge at dusk and run along deserted shores or down lonely roads.

Probably the most famous historical account of 'Black Shuck' occurred in the sixteenth century at Bungay on the borders of Norfolk and Suffolk. It was on Sunday, 4 August 1557 that the animal made a somewhat out of character appearance on the outskirts of the town and loped up the main street. The area was deserted at the time, for most of the people were at church celebrating evensong, and whether attracted by the singing or simply by design, the dog entered the building.

The sudden appearance of the animal surrounded by 'fearful flashes of fire' to quote a pamphlet, *The Demon of Bungay*, published in 1558, immediately threw the congregation into panic. And in the ensuing mêlée, 'Old Shuck' left two worshippers dead and another man 'as shrunken as a piece of leather scorched in a hot fire', according to the same source.

Whether the members of the congregation actually died from being attacked by the dog or were victims of the mad scramble to get out of its way has never been definitely established. What is known is that the demon raced away from the town, and that same evening was reported again twelve miles away at the fifteenth century church of the Holy Trinity in Blytheburgh. Here he once more entered the church packed with worshippers and caused the death of a man and a boy.

After this second attack, the creature disappeared into the night and was heard of no more, according to the pamphlet, although there were those who could still not quite believe the evidence of their own eyes, wondering if it had actually been a dog or 'the Devil in such a likeness.'

Despite the terror of this visitation by 'Black Shuck', it is interesting to discover that Suffolk people by and large believe the dog to be fairly harmless if he is left alone – though he can kill if approached too closely. Two sightings this century would seem to substantiate this belief.

The first occurred in the early 1900's in the churchyard at Leiston, a small community in the shadow of the famous Sizewell nuclear plant which dominates the coastline between Aldeburgh and Southwold. The eye-witnesses were a certain Lady Rendlesham and a friend who actually went to the church one midnight to see if there was any truth in the local legend about a demon hound haunting the vicinity. They were not disappointed either, as Lady Rendlesham declared later:

At twelve o'clock precisely, a slinking, sable shadow slipped among the gravestones like a wraith, leaped the low churchyard wall and slid down the dark lane toward the sandhills like an evil whisper. We saw 'The Galleytrot' [another term sometimes used in Suffolk for 'Old Shuck'] and lived to tell the tale!

In fact, neither of the two ladies believed they would be harmed by the creature, but friends and relatives who had tried to dissuade them from their investigation were very relieved to see them returning home unharmed as the sun rose over Leiston.

The second encounter occurred in 1938 when a Mr Ernest Whiteland of Ditchingham saw the animal make a return appearance in Bungay. His account is notable for its careful attention to detail.

It was an early autumn evening and I was making my way home. I had been spending the evening with friends at a reading room in Bungay. As I crossed Bungay market-place, the clock of St Mary's Church was striking ten. I went down Bridge Street and across Ditchingham Dam, turned to the right past the Maltings, which used to be a silk factory, and was about halfway between the foreman's house at the Maltings and Ditchingham Station, when I saw a black object roughly seventy-five yards away, coming towards me. I was on the lefthand side of the road, close to the hedge.

As it came close, I could see it was a large black dog, trotting along the same side of the road as I was on. It was a lovely evening – no wind, and everything was so quiet and still. As it came to about nine or ten yards away, I could see that it had a long, black, shaggy coat, and was about 28 to 30 inches tall. I moved into the middle of the road to let it pass. When it got level with me, it vanished!

I looked round to see if I had made a mistake, to see if it was still running along, but could not see it. I then went and looked over the hedge, expecting to see it on the meadow, or hear it, but could do neither. I stopped, it seemed to me, for some minutes. Then a sudden fear came over me, and it did not take me long to cover the distance to my home.

The next day I told some of my friends about my experience and they told me I had seen Black Shuck which everybody in the locality knew about and which many had seen. I have since been past that place lots of times and at all hours, but I have not seen or heard anything more.

In Norfolk, however, the attitude of the people towards the demon dog is quite different, as local historian Tom Dodd of West Runton has explained.

The Norfolk Shuck is an awful creature, as black as ebony and his fiendish howls can be heard above even the wildest storm. There are lots of stories of people sensing 'Black Shuck' padding up behind them and feeling his icy breath on the back of their necks. Even today, motorists have reported swerving to avoid the demon dog crossing the road.

Tom says that there is a popular belief that no-one can set eyes on the dog and live, and among some country folk there is also a general term used about anyone who is dying that 'the black dog is at his, or her, heels.'

This historian believes that 'Black Shuck' has quite a lot in common with the werewolves who once used to haunt the sparsely populated areas of East Anglia, and it was in support of this claim that he gave me a copy of a story about a demon dog which I reproduce hereunder. In it the reader will see certain aspects of the creature's behaviour that make it appear very like one of Black Shuck's progeny. The report was published in the *Norfolk News* in 1895 and is of even greater interest to our story because the location is said to be a spot on the coast near Cromer.

This tale is common talk among the beachmen, and concerns a gentleman of very dark complexion and curly hair, who, it transpires, asked a fisher-boy to look after a dog for him, as he was going away. Now, the dog had been seen in the town, and its ownership was well known, though, strange to say, the dog and his master had never been seen together. It was a fine dog, a large, curly black retriever, very long and lean.

When the fisher-boy found that the gentleman had indeed gone away, he began to look after the dog, for which he had been very handsomely paid beforehand.

Every morning the boy, who was fourteen years old, went out to swim in the sea and the dog went with him. One day, when the boy had swum further than usual, he found that the dog savagely resented his returning to shore, with such growlings and menaces, that the terrified boy was obliged to swim on and on, still further out to sea, whilst the dog swam close behind him.

At last, the boy turning his head round in desperation, saw to his intense and almost benumbing terror, the dark, saturnine face of the dark-complexioned and curly-haired gentleman close behind him – the metamorphosis was only momentary, and on looking round again he saw the dog had re-appeared, and by continued and fierce growling and biting still urged him out to sea. Fortunately, a smack, under press of sail, scudded by, and the boy was able to attract the notice of those on board, who came to his rescue, but his neck and shoulder were bleeding from the dog's angry attack. The animal was seen to dive like a porpoise, and, re-appearing a great distance off, swam away.

After the remarkable escape above recorded, it was remembered, on all sides, how many boys about fourteen years old were yearly drowned off the coast, and how, in particular, only a year or so back, a boy's body had been found washed up off Runton Point, with the marks of a dog's teeth on the neck and shoulder, which till now had been placed to the credit of an attempt to save the life on the part of some noble animal.

A more recent clipping that Tom Dodd also brought to my attention provided a description of 'Black Shuck' in his traditional setting on land. It came from the files of the *East Anglian Daily Times* of 25 May 1939 and concerned the frightening experience of a Norfolk man named Jimmy Farman who had met the hound on the marshes near St Olive's while walking with his own dog.

A great black dog it was, and the eyes were like railway lamps. He crossed my path down by the dyke and my old bitch almost went mad with fear. Crouched down she did, and the hairs rose up on her back as though they were bristles. For some minutes I couldn't get her to move; no, not a step; and she moaned terribly, just like a child.

Tom Dodd is one of several folklore experts who believe that the coast around Cromer has the longest and best documented association with 'Black Shuck'. One of these is another Norfolk man, John Harries, who wrote in his *Ghost Hunter's Road Book* (1968):

> Those bold enough to search for this spectral beast cannot do better than to travel the A149 between Hunstanton and Cromer. To know this wild and lovely coast on which the Vikings landed and gave the villages of today their names, one has to stop and walk around. East of Sheringham there are cliffs extending to Cromer. This is one of the favourite haunts of Black Shuck. The road runs fairly close to the coastline, and there are paths along the top of the cliffs. Local inhabitants prefer to stick to the road if walking back to Sheringham or Cromer to their homes around West Runton. And the reason is not that they are afraid of falling over the cliff...

Mr Harries believes that the route most used by the Hell Hound is alongside the path which starts near Cromer lighthouse and leads to Overstand.

> He prefers a night when the wind is so strong that it is hardly possible to stand erect, and only the fact that it is blowing from the sea makes it safe to force oneself forward on one's way. 'Black Shuck' is essentially a dog of the sea. He serves his purpose as a warning. If he is abroad then the storms are bad and fishermen would be wise to heed the supernatural sign that they will get worse. To their womenfolk the dog gives the ominous news that the sea may be exacting its toll of another human life before dawn comes.

Further support for this claim can be found in W.A. Dutt's excellent book, *Highways and Byways in East Anglia* (1923). In it the author discusses another element to the legend – that the demon dog sometimes has only one eye:

If it is a stormy night instead of a stormy day, the old fisher folk of the coast will say it is just the time for 'Black Shuck' to be abroad, for he revels in the roaring of the waves and loves to raise his awful voice above the howling of the gale. You may know him at once, should you see him, by his fiery eye; he has but one, and that, like the Cyclops, is in the middle of his head. But such an encounter might bring you the worst of luck; it is even said that to meet him is to be warned that your death will occur before the end of the year. So you will do well to shut your eyes if you hear him howling – shut them even if you are uncertain whether it is the dog-fiend or the voice of the wind you hear.

One person who was in no doubt she had heard – and seen – the 'dog-fiend' was Annie Thurston, who lived not far from Lowestoft and recounted her dramatic encounter to a folklkore expert, Morley Adams, about fifty years ago. Annie was a pretty young girl and was out walking one evening with her fiancé, Josh, when the events that she so vividly describes occurred.

It was between eight and nine and we were in a lane near Geldeston where we met Mrs. S. and she started to walk with us. Then I heard something behind us, like the sound of a dog running. I thought it was some farmer's dog, and paid little attention to it, but it kept on just at the back of us, pit-pat-pit-pat-pit-pat!

'I wonder what that dog wants,' I said to Mrs S.

'What dog do you mean?' said she, looking all around.

'Why, can't you hear it?' I said, 'it has been following us for the last five minutes or more! You can hear it, can't you, Josh?' I said.

'Nonsense, old mawther,' said Josh, 'just you lug hold of my arm and come along.'

I was walking between Josh and Mrs. S. and I laid hold of Mrs S's arm and she said, 'I can hear it now; it's in front of us; look, there it be!' And sure enough just in front of us was what looked like a big, black dog; but it wasn't a dog at all; it was the Hell Hound that had been seen hereabouts before and it betokened some great misfortune. It kept right in front of us until it came to the churchyard, when it went right through the wall and we saw it no more.

Morley Adams who later investigated the story to satisfy himself of its veracity, found others who confirmed Annie Thurston's account. They also told him that as long as those being followed showed no fear of Shuck he would just pad silently behind – though if a person turned round 'the beast would growl and snarl like a mad dog.' According to these country-folk the creature had been known to drag children along the road by their clothes, and dire disaster always overtook any individual who persisted in running away.

Morley Adams concluded his report, 'The people who are most likely to see the Hell Hound are those born under the chime hours, or towards the small hours of Friday night.'

One final personal encounter cited by Alasdair Alpin MacGregor in his *Ghost Book* (1955) should also be included because of its reference yet again to Cromer. Mr MacGregor writes:

> One evening at the turn of the century, Mr. and Mrs. Reynolds of Southwold when driving home along the road near Reydon Hall, also saw Black Shuck. It seemed almost under their horses' hooves. 'Mother called out,' Miss Mildred Reynolds tells me, 'and father took whip to frighten it, so they should not run it over – and it just wasn't there any longer!'
>
> Many years later, when Mrs. Reynolds happened to mention this terrifying experience to Miss Wilmer, a relative of the owner of Reydon Hall, she learnt for the first time of Black Shuck, the phantom so often encountered on the road between Aldeburgh and Cromer, and nearly always before a spell of rough weather.

It is perhaps not surprising, therefore, in the light of all this evidence that Sir Arthur Conan Doyle should have been fascinated by the dog and ultimately woven it into a great story. Nor should it come as any more of a surprise to learn that the beauty of the East Anglian coast with its rich store of legends drew him back time and again and provided the inspiration for another case for Sherlock Holmes.

The setting this time was the lonely stretch of coastline around the little community of Happisburgh, which has the reputation of being haunted by one of the most gruesome spectres on record. The ghost is said to be that of a legless smuggler whose appearance is made all the more hideous because his head hangs down backwards between his shoulders and is only attached to his neck by a thin strip of skin.

Happisburgh, which is called locally 'Hasboro', is also well-known for the sand-banks off the coast referred to as 'Hasboro Sands' which, according to W.A. Dutt, 'have taken a terrible toll of those who go down to the sea in ships.' He continues:

> Hundreds of vessels have gone to pieces on that dreaded sand-bank, and thousands of lives have been lost, despite the heroic efforts of the lifeboatmen and the crews of the North Sea trawlers. No record has been kept of the Hasboro shipwrecks; even in recent years they have been so many that the lifeboatmen have not kept count of them.

Mr Dutt says that the neighbourhood was also popular with smugglers for their nefarious activities.

> But only in East Norfolk could it occur to these 'freetraders' to take advantage of the general credulity in respect of Old Shuck by tying a lantern to a dog or a donkey to scare away inquisitive people by making them think that the canine phantom was pursuing them!

The ghost of the monstrous smuggler was a quite different matter, however, according to E.A. Suffling in *History and Legends of the Broad District* (1890). The phantom was apparently regularly seen in the early 1800's carrying a large sack in its arms as it progressed from the sea to a place in the village known as Well Corner. On reaching this spot, the ghost invariably disappeared, and it was here that the first bold investigators carried out their search. Imagine the horror when one of them was lowered by a rope into the well and discovered a sack containing a man's torso from which the head and legs had been severed! Mr Suffling writes:

> A week or two after this discovery, evidence was obtained that a sailor had been murdered near the Cart Gap, where a pool of blood was discovered, and, in a shed near by, a pistol that matched one found on the decapitated body. Some gold pieces were also found embedded in the earth, and fragments of three empty 'Schiedam Bottles' strewn about. From all this, it was deduced that a party of Dutch smugglers had landed on the coast where they had caroused and quarrelled, and one of their number had been killed by having his head nearly severed from his body. It had been the man's restless ghost that had brought about the discovery of his remains.

Though I have no specific evidence that Conan Doyle heard this grisly tale during his stay at Hill House Hotel in Happisburgh, he certainly *did* find there the idea for the story, *Adventure of the Dancing Men*.

At the time of the author's visit to Happisburgh, the Sherlock Holmes cases had already made their author famous, and he was quite used to being proffered autograph books to sign. This happened when the young son of the proprietor of Hill House, a man named G J Cubitt, politely asked for his signature. As Doyle leafed through the book to find a suitable page, his eye apparently alighted on a signature and address which had been written in the form of several 'dancing men'. The cipher excited his imagination and he was soon devising a case for Holmes which featured the discovery of a secret message written in similar hieroglyphics.

To acknowledge his debt to Happisburgh and its little hotel, Conan Doyle not only featured the village in *Adventure of the Dancing Men* – as well as two other nearby places, Walcott and North Walham – but actually named the central character Hilton Cubitt. His own satisfaction with the story was later made clear when he placed it third in his list of 'the twelve best adventures of Sherlock Holmes.'

I, too, have cause to remember Happisburgh. For it was

while I was there looking, out of interest, for Riding Thorpe Manor, the home of Hilton Cubitt (which some Sherlockians actually believe to be in one or other of the two neighbouring villages of Ridlington or Edingthorp), that I had the second of the strange experiences which occurred while I was investigating the story of the Norfolk Hell Hound.

I was walking down a narrow lane when I was suddenly conscious of the sound of heavy breathing coming up behind me. I turned round just as a man on horseback galloped past. The rider was crouched low over the animal and, in the half light of a winter's afternoon, both man and beast seemed almost like one. The blackness of the animal and the virtual lack of noise from its hooves as it galloped over the sodden bank of the lane, dramatically brought to my mind all that I had learned about 'Black Shuck'. Even stranger, it reminded me of a paragraph in a book that I had read at the very start of my research into the subject.

The book was *Haunted East Anglia* by Joan Forman, and I turned to it again with the experiences on Cromer Beach and at Happisburgh still fresh in my memory. It did not provide me with the answer to the legend of 'Black Shuck' – not that I had expected it would – but it certainly gave me food for thought, and I should like to close this section by quoting Miss Forman's intriguing remarks and leave the reader to ponder them further for himself.

In Norfolk the phantom animal is known as 'Old Shuck', though in other parts of England he has other names, the best known being that of the trash or padfoot. I suspect that in cases where a similar ghost appears in many widely-scattered areas, the apparition is not an echo of a life lived on earth, but is a racial or archetypal memory, perhaps of a one-time religious fetish or object of reverence in pagan days. Certainly the padfoot reaches right back in time – as far, at least, as the Scottish Kelpie or the Irish Banshee. Such visual creations are planted deep in the imagination of the race, handed down hereditarily in some part of the unconscious mind in a manner not yet understood. At what point the memory derived from actual event, it is impossible to tell. There are many buried facts which the race rather than the individual remembers. Giants and dragons, for instance, now thought to be imaginative creations, may at one time have been realities for our remote ancestors. So, perhaps, with 'Old Shuck', a giant dog with staring eyes. The earliest known horses were about the size of giant dogs. An idea, only – I await a better one.

# 4   The Sea Serpent of Kessingland

One of the biggest attractions for young holidaymakers on the East Anglian coast is undoubtedly the Pleasurewood Hills theme park just to the north of Lowestoft. This American-style fun centre with its mixture of over fifty fascinating exhibits and breathtaking rides (including the rattlesnake coaster looking for all the world like a giant sea serpent as it twists and turns through the air) offers visitors a day of thrills and excitement.

Just to the south of Lowestoft, however, there is the chance of a very different kind of excitement for anyone who chooses to spend some time looking for what is said to be a real life version of the Loch Ness Monster. For according to a local tradition and a number of eye-witness accounts, there is a sea serpent in the water off Kessingland Beach. And if you add to these stories another intriguing legend of a monster like a man who was actually caught by some fishermen of Orford, it is plain that this is another area of the 'supernatural coast' worthy of investigation.

At first glance, Kessingland seems little different to many other seaside communities around the coast. There is a fine, wide beach with a shingle bank often covered by small boats and families of holidaymakers. What is not immediately evident – but is a source of pride to local people – is that the beach was one of forty-eight seaside resorts around Britain which were awarded the European Commission's highest accolade for consumer-friendly bathing in June 1991. Along with a number of other much more famous beaches at places like Bridlington, Eastbourne, Bournemouth, Weymouth, Paignton and Weston-super-Mare, Kessingland earned a Golden Starfish Award for its pollution-free sea. (The major beaches were actually awarded blue flags, but as Kessingland was deemed too small to qualify for this, it and twelve other similar tiny resorts got the Golden Starfish.)

Despite such recognition, it is still true that Kessingland has for years been an attraction during high summer to overspill holidaymakers from Lowestoft and Great Yarmouth. There is also another popular draw in the shape of the Suffolk Wildlife and Country Park on the outskirts of the Village, just off the A12. Indeed, the variety of animals and birds such as timber wolves, wallabies, black swans and sacred ibis, all in their natural surroundings, offer a fascinating interlude for all nature lovers.

But those who are intrigued by the mysterious are more likely to be drawn to the sea and the chance of a glimpse of the monster – or at least to get an account of it from a local fisherman.

The relentless tides and fast-flowing currents, which are as active on this stretch of coast as anywhere else on England's eastern seaboard, have left their mark on the beaches where long, desolate strips of mud, sand, clay and shingle provide the visible evidence of the sea's power. This continual battle with the elements has, in fact, resulted in the sea pushing back the land frontier by no less than a quarter of a mile during the past 400 years, all along the coast from Kessingland to the busy port of Felixstowe in the south.

To the north of the resort, there is an almost unbroken line of impressive cliffs – though nowhere are they higher than 70ft – running as far as Lowestoft, which are of special interest to lovers of scenic landscapes and geologists. Indeed, they are arguably the most imposing stretch of cliffs to be seen along the entire Suffolk coast and have rightly been declared an 'area of outstanding natural beauty'. Curiosity seekers might also find interest in one of the clefts or 'gaps' just to the north of the resort which is known locally as 'Crazy Mary's Hole' – the story being that it was frequented for years by a lovesick girl who went mad after her lover was drowned at sea.

It is, however, because of the numerous geological finds that have been made here that Kessingland has a special interest for geologists. Let the local historian W.A. Dutt explain:

> On the pages of the stratigraphical record preserved here, the geologist finds imprinted a story reading almost like a romance: for it tells him that ages ago, when England was united with the Continent of Europe by land covering a part of the area now occupied by the North Sea, the river now known as the Rhine flowed as far westward as Kessingland where it turned northward and followed more or less closely the trend of the present coast-line as far as Cromer.

The constant erosion of the waves against the cliffs has exposed all sorts of treasures from the past, Mr Dutt goes on:

> Tree trunks and the bones of extinct animals have been brought to light, all, or nearly all, of them showing signs of having been washed down to the place where they were found by the waters of the great river which left them stranded on the ooze flats which had formed at a bend of its course.
>
> Remains of two extinct species of elephant, the cave bear, the giant elk, and three species of rhinoceros are among the relics of the fauna that inhabited the shores of the river in this long-gone age, while from the seeds and leaves found preserved in the oozey stratum of the Forest Bed the botanist is able to tell what kind of vegetation grew by the riverside and on the bordering marshes.
>
> Years ago, before the falling of the cliffs had covered most of the Forest Bed deposits with sand and masses of Boulder Clay, two or three old beachmen were always on the look-out for fossilised bones of the wonderful animals which, as the old men would say, 'lived before the Flood'.

What more likely spot, therefore, for a species of sea monster to live that might well date from the earliest times?

Quite when stories of the sea monster at Kessingland first began to be discussed is now impossible to determine, but certainly there is evidence of oral tales of a creature 'with a long neck and a head much like that of a seal' being handed down among local families for several centuries. The earliest written account dates from the year 1750 and appears in the form of a report in that treasury of the unusual, *The Gentleman's Magazine.*

In the December issue there is an account of a monster said to have been seen off the Suffolk coast at Kessingland. 'The creature was about five feet long from what could be viewed of it above the water,' the magazine stated, 'with a head like a dog and a beard like a lion. The skin was spotted like that of a leopard. It passed in a leisurely fashion, finally disappearing beneath the waves to the great amazement of all those watching from the shore.'

It has been suggested by some experts that the creature may well have been a type of seal – but the eye-witnesses, all local people, were familiar with such creatures, and in any event were also quite used to seeing unusual and unexpected creatures such as rorqual whales in the sea.

It is about the middle of the nineteenth century that there are more persistent accounts of a creature with 'a head such as a serpent might have with humps behind' swimming through the waves about a hundred yards from the Kessingland beach. However, the most dramatic eye-witness account I have been able to trace is that of a young girl and her two companions who saw the creature one summer day in 1912. The girl was Lilias Rider Haggard, the daughter of the famous novelist Sir Henry Rider Haggard, who himself later vouched for the authenticity of their account.

Sir Henry, (1856-1925) well remembered to this day for his classic novels of high adventure such as *King Solomon's Mines* and *She*, was born in Norfolk and spent many summers with his family at his coastal retreat, Kessingland Grange, overlooking the sea. This house near the cliff edge had once been a famous resort of smugglers but was later commandeered to be used in the fight against them as a coastguard station, before finally becoming a private residence.

Rider Haggard was a man who had travelled widely and experienced the fantastic in many forms – particularly in Africa – yet admitted he had heard of nothing stranger than the story of the Kessingland sea serpent. It was a story he found difficult to believe until he was presented with an account of the monster by none other than his own daughter, Lilias.

The famous author was actually working on a novel at his home in Ditchingham, about fifteen miles from the coast, when he received a letter from Lilias at Kessingland Grange, dated 20 July 1912. He read the lines which follow with mounting amazement.

We had a great excitement here this evening, and we are convinced we have seen a sea serpent! I happened to look up when I was sitting on the lawn, and saw what looked like a thin, dark line with a blob at one end, shooting through the water at such a terrific speed it hardly seemed possible anything alive could go at such a pace. It was some way out over the sandbank, and travelling parallel with the shore. I tore into the morning room and got the glasses and though it had at that moment nearly vanished in the distance we could make out it had a sort of head at one end and then a series of about 30 pointed blobs which dwindled in size as they neared the tail. As it went along it seemed to get more and more submerged and then vanished. You can't imagine the pace it was going. I suppose it was about 60 feet long.

As Rider Haggard read this letter all thought of his novel slipped from his mind. His daughter was not by nature a practical joker nor prone to imaginative flights of fantasy. She had clearly been deeply impressed by what she had seen and now wanted an explanation. The author decided to travel to Kessingland Grange at once.

Lilias Haggard was still bubbling with excitement about what she had seen when her father arrived at the Grange. Once more she went over what she had seen, pointing out of the window to precisely where the creature had appeared. Had it been a sea serpent, she asked?

Rider Haggard admitted he was puzzled and summoned a couple of his servants, the cook and a gardener. Both were Kessingland folk and had already heard Lilias's account.

'No doubt about it,' the man answered, nodding his head. 'The young missie has seen the sea serpent. They've talked about it here for years. Turns up in the summer looking for a mate, some say.'

The cook also nodded her head in agreement. 'My father was a fisherman and he used to say it was as big as a trawler, all covered in scales. It's got a head like the sea serpents you see in old picture books.

News of this sighting soon spread throughout Kessingland, and although no-one else could be found to corroborate Lilias Haggard's report, her father decided to write to the local newspaper, the *Eastern Daily Press*, enclosing a copy of her letter. Such a missive from an ordinary member of the public might well have been treated with some cynicism by the editor – but no-one could question the probity of one of England's leading novelists.

So, on the morning of Wednesday 24 July, Lilias's letter appeared under the heading 'Sea Serpent off Kessingland' accompanied by the following note from Rider Haggard:

> Sir – In the hope that it may elicit an explanation, I enclose a portion of a letter received from my daughter who is staying at my house, Kessingland Grange, near Lowestoft. May I ask: (1) Has anybody else seen a peculiar creature in the sea off the East Coast? and (2) Could what my daughter and her two companions saw have been a school of porpoises travelling at a great rate?'

It was typical of Haggard that he should propose a rational explanation for the extraordinary sighting – and, indeed, several letters sent to the paper declared the 'monster' must have been either a school of porpoises or dolphins, though such are rarely seen in the chilly North Sea.

Alternatively, it could have been a sand-bank suddenly exposed by the waves. One correspondent maintained it was simply a trick of the early evening light.

Two writers, however, reiterated the old legend of the Kessingland sea serpent and were in no doubt that this was what the girl had seen. One of these, a Mr R.V. Shelton of Great Yarmouth, wrote, 'We are always being told that such monsters are the creatures of legend and should be dismissed as such. The evidence of young Miss Haggard disputes such a statement and reminds us that we should not close our minds to what we cannot readily explain.'

My own research has also uncovered two further sightings of the sea serpent to underline the story – in 1923 and 1978 respectively.

The first was provided by Captain F.E.B. Haselfoot, the captain of a survey ship, H M Kellett, which was taking observations off the Norfolk coast in August 1923. He and the ship's navigator, Lt.Commander R.M. Southern, were suddenly startled to see a creature with a long neck rising from the waves. Captain Haselfoot later wrote:

> The time was about 9 a.m. It was a summer day and the weather was calm and clear. I am not sure whether the sun was actually shining. I then observed rising out of the water about 200 yards from the ship, a long, serpentine neck, projecting from six to seven feet above the water. I observed this neck rising out of the water twice, and it remained up, in each case, for four or five seconds. Viewing with the naked eye only, I could not make out precisely what the head was like.

Captain Haselfoot said that he was unable to attract the attention of his colleague until the neck was appearing for the second time. Lt.Commander Southern could not distinguish the features of the head either, but estimated that it was about eight to ten ft up from the surface of the water. Both men, accustomed as they were to making accurate observations at sea, were in no doubt as to what they had seen. Like Lilias Haggard, Captain Haselfoot made a quick sketch of the monster which has also survived to this day.

The most recent sighting, in July 1978, was made by a holidaymaker on Kessingland beach as he was walking in the direction of Covehithe. The man, who asked to remain anonymous when he provided details for the *East Anglian Magazine* later in the year, stated:

> The sea was quite calm when my attention was suddenly drawn to what I can only say looked like the head of a seal on a long neck sticking up out of the water. There seemed to be some humps behind the head, but the creature only remained visible for a matter of a few seconds before diving beneath the surface. I would be inclined to think that I had imagined everything if I had not read the story of the Kessingland Sea Serpent.

For students of sea mysteries, this story no doubt holds as much interest as the puzzling case of the creature which was actually pulled from the sea a few miles down the coast at Orford Ness. The report of the man-like monster caught in the year 1204 is not only continuing to draw interested visitors to the area, but has been celebrated in ballads, poems, essays and most recently a book,*The Wildman*, by the excellent East Anglian historian, Kevin Crossley-Holland.

Today, the fact that Orford was once an important community in East Anglia can really only be gauged by visiting the magnificent castle with its three turrets and outstanding views from the battlements. The 90 ft high building was erected in 1165 by Henry II to exercise his royal prerogative in what was then a rather unsettled and troublesome part of his kingdom. At the time, Orford was itself a thriving seaport, and the spit of shingle stretching six miles south-west along which holidaymakers now wander, used to end near the quay. Its gradual extension brought about by the action of the tides finally cut off the community from the sea however. Now Orford looks rather like any typical East Anglian village except for the road leading down to the quay.

There are two other prominent landmarks to be seen: the red and white lighthouse on Orford Ness, and on the foreshore various Ministry of Defence structures which are a subject of wry comment by the locals. Indeed, when I first came to the area looking for information about the fabled thirteenth century sea monster, I was soon treated to a local joke.

'You want to know about a monster?' one old salt working on his boat on the shingle smiled at me. 'Well, I'll tell you. See all that scientific jiggery-pokery over there? That's the real Orford Ness monster!'

Once the fisherman had had his little joke, however, he was happy to outline the basic story of the 'merman' – as he called the creature – and referred me to a book in which I would find all the details.

The main source of information about the creature is, in fact, a volume entitled *The Suffolk Traveller* published in 1821 by the English entomologist, William Kirby (1759-1850), who was born at Witnesham Hall, Suffolk, and devoted his life to the study of wildlife. Admittedly, though, he drew on earlier sources to provide the information about what is surely one of the strangest objects ever fished from the sea.

There is a story that, in or around the year 1204, a sea monster resembling a man in size and figure was caught by the fishermen of Orford in their nets. He had hair on those parts of the body where it usually grows, except on the crown of his head, which was bald, and his beard was long and ragged.

According to the historian, the man-fish was presented to the governor of Orford Castle and was kept tied up there to prevent him escaping. It was said that he ate both fish and meat, either raw or cooked, 'though when raw he first pressed it in his hands.'

The unfortunate creature was apparently cruelly tortured by servants in the castle who tied his hands and feet and poked and hit him to try to make him speak. It was also said that he lay down to sleep as soon as the sun set and got up immediately at dawn. Kirby continues:

> One day, the fishermen carried him to the sea and there let him go, having first spread three rows of strong nets to prevent his escape. But diving under them, he appeared beyond their barriers, and seemed to deride his astonished keepers who, giving him up for lost, returned home – wither they were soon followed by the monster who continued to live with them for some time. But being, it is said, weary of living alone, he stole away to sea one night and was heard of no more.

William Kirby found himself unable to dismiss the story as an idle invention, though other writers in the intervening years have claimed it to be a mere fable. The entomologist, for his part, was well aware of the stories of strange creatures that had been reported over the years on the East Anglian coast and felt there was so much detail in the tale that it had a ring of authenticity about it.

At the turn of this century, W.A. Dutt also spent some time investigating the legend and agreed with the facts as outlined by Kirby. But he added one further new and intriguing piece of information.

> It has been alleged that this story may have had its origin in the keeping of a pet seal in the castle, and there have been some writers unkind enough to suggest that the monster was a captive priest. But my own enquiries have discovered that there is still a tradition that the wild man of Orford occasionally makes an appearance in lonely parts of the coast.

Who or what the Orford Ness monster was (or may even still be, if we accept Mr Dutt's word!) is certainly going to be difficult to establish, but his legend is already assured not only in books like *The Wildman* by Kevin Crossley-Holland (1976), but in several pubs in East Anglia named 'The Green Man', on whose signs he is depicted. One of the best of these examples is appropriately to be found at Kessingland.

A curious footnote to the legend has been provided by an East Anglian writer, Rowena Groom. She was told by her father that the 'green man' illustrated on the inn signs was actually based on a creature caught by fishermen 'off Kessingland, north of Covehithe' sometime about the end of the eighteenth century. The naked fellow was apparently taken on shore, fed and clothed, and gradually absorbed into the community.

In time, says Rowena Groom, the 'green man' found a girl he wished to marry and settle down with – but on the very day of their wedding he suddenly disappeared never to be seen again. Had he returned to the sea? No-one ever found out. But according to the story, the girl later gave birth to a child with a distinctly greenish hue, and to this day any baby born along this stretch of coast with a noticeably sallow skin is whispered to be 'of the green man's progeny'...

# 5  'The Walberswick Whisperers'

The ferry ride across the River Blyth from the town of Southwold to the little village of Walberswick provides another opportunity to undertake one of the East Anglian coast's several journeys back in time. Although it is certainly true that Southwold on its rolling cliff top has retained a kind of old-fashioned graciousness, Walberswick – eight miles away for travellers by road, but a few minutes in a ferry-boat across a couple of hundred yards of waterway – seems forever locked in the past.

Years ago Walberswick was a flourishing port, but the pounding North Sea destroyed the harbour by continually blocking and shifting the outlet of the river. None the less, it is popular today with small boat sailors, though they have to contend with a muddy foreshore and those constant strong currents.

The village itself offers idyllic views across heathland, reed-filled marshes and the sea. By day, the colours of the countryside are beautifully soft and muted, and over the years the place has attracted a great many painters, birdwatchers, walkers and golfers. By night, though, it is a very different story: for this is the domain of 'The Walberswick Whisperers'...

Catching the last ferry across the Blyth, as evening begins to fall and the boatman is obviously wanting to finish, can be a strange experience which mixes the picturesque with the uncanny. As the fading sun turns the shades of the landscape darker and then plunges them into shadow, the ferryman's oars gently slap in and out of the water and the sound is heightened by the stillness all around. The man himself stands in the bows of his small craft rather like the ferryman of the Styx, equally as upright, sombre and silent as the figure of legend.

It was, in fact, only as the boat landed on the Walberswick side that he finally answered the enquiry I had put to him earlier about the legend of the 'Whisperers'.

'Some nights hereabouts,' he said as he shipped his oars and tied the ferry up against the small jetty, 'the sky looks sort of sinister. What you'd call supernatural. [He pronounced it soopy-natural]. That's the sign for the spirits to rise up with the wind and start a mutterin'. All shapes and sizes they are, chatterin' and sighin'. We call them the "Walberswick Whisperers". You want to know any more, go and talk to some of they folk in the village.'

Having said this, the ferryman fell silent and turned on his heels and was soon gone into the gathering gloom. He was clearly not prepared to answer any more of the questions I had about the ghosts of Walberswick – in particular about the ferry's phantom passengers. 'Soopy-natural' beings were evidently not things he wanted to discuss when a good hot meal was awaiting him...

The neat-looking Anchor Hotel in the centre of the village which was my first port of call proved to be only one place from which I subsequently gathered stories about the phenomena known as the 'Walberswick Whispers'. Stories which included a mysterious man and his young companion waiting to catch the ferry, a wailing spirit that haunted the old vicarage and the ghost of a miser believed to stride about the Common. Plus a phantom animal, the spectre of a soldier called Black Toby, and a haunted inn where the mysterious behaviour of some bedclothes may have inspired one of the finest modern ghost stories. And, perhaps most extraordinary of all, a suggestion that the 'Whisperers' might now have spread their influence beyond this remote locality to within a few miles of the busy port of Lowestoft...

It was appropriately a local fisherman who I met in the bar of the Anchor who explained the legend of the phantom ferry passengers which I could not extract from the boatman – a story which, he insisted, was familiar to many folk.

The haunting apparently came to general attention earlier this century when a visitor to Walberswick asked Old Todd, who was then the ferryman, to row him over to the Southwold side. As the man approached the small boat he passed the figures of an old man holding a small child by the hand. Seating himself in the boat, the visitor was surprised to see that Old Todd was about to pull away from the shore without the other two passengers. He suggested that the ferryman wait for them and turned round to see where the pair might be.

To his amazement, there was no sign of either – and as the boatman began to row he said quietly, almost under his breath, 'We never wait for *them*!'

The visitor later discovered that the two phantoms had been reported on a number of previous occasions and were well-known in the district. But quite who they might be and why they could not get onto the ferry was a mystery. A local resident, Miss Helen Palmer, contributed further confirmation of the haunting to an anthology, *The Ghost Book*, published locally in the early fifties, in which she wrote:

> On several occasions while waiting for the ferry I saw an old man holding by the hand a small boy. On the first occasion I, too, drew the ferryman's attention to them, thinking he had not noticed their approach. 'They *never* cross!' whispered the ferryman, shrugging his shoulders and with a meaningful tone in his voice.

The ferry is also the subject of a second ghost story which is described in the same collection and I quote it verbatim:

> Close to the ferry on the Walberswick side stood a house known locally as the Old Vicarage. It functioned as a guest house until a bomb demolished it during the Second World War. The story goes that it was once occupied by an unfortunate Walberswick woman who bore a large number of children, only one of whom survived infancy. But in her distraction, the mother killed this surviving infant lest it

should suffer or be taken from her. After the mother herself died, it was said that her ghost was heard seeking her lost children, wailing and crying through the old house. A spiritualist who stayed there shortly before the bomb fell was said to have tried to exorcise the mournful ghost, but whether he succeeded or the German bomb completed the task is unknown.

It is, however, the Common in Walberswick that is most beset by phantoms if all the stories I collected are anything to go by. Indeed, it was an account of one of these, by the author Penelope Fitzgerald, which first prompted my interest in the village and made me decide to visit it.

Miss Fitzgerald's story of her supernatural experience particularly caught my interest because of her admission that she had previously been a sceptic about ghosts. However, she had subsequently come to believe that spirits are not necessarily frightening and that the majority of people do not actually recognize them as such when they first see them. The realization that someone has had a brush with the paranormal, she maintains, does not come until later. She explains her own encounter in a very matter-of-fact manner.

It happened while I was living in Walberswick. I was taking a pony across the common when it jibbed absolutely at passing what looked to me like four large milk bottles in the bracken. When we got closer, I saw it was a white dog like a very large pointer, and it was only later that I thought it strange that the dog could lope away through the bracken without a sound. When I made some enquiries in the village about what I had seen I was told that the dog was a well-known haunter. It was said to have been seen 'waiting for somebody' on the common for at least the past one hundred years.

Another vivid account of an animal phantom haunting the Common has been provided by Helen Palmer, who wrote as follows:

My terrifying experience occurred on a sunny September morning while I was blackberrying on the Common. I remember that a cold wind suddenly sprang up about me and I heard distinctly the sound of galloping hooves, growing louder and louder as if approaching me. I looked all around, but could see nothing except the rough grass, the bushes and the blue, untroubled sky. Nonetheless, I took to my heels and made for home. Neighbours to whom I afterwards confided told me that they never crossed that particular bit of land. There was 'an evil haunt' on it, they said.

It has been suggested to me that both of these haunts may have been the handiwork of 'Black Shuck' on the prowl, although in no other account is he described as being white or making the noise of 'galloping hooves' with his paws. There is, though, one seemingly genuine account of his appearance in Walberswick recorded by the author Alasdair Alpin MacGregor.

'I once experienced the terrible monster of the Common' a Walberswick lady told me, 'and only once, and that was quite enough.' It transpired that she and her sister-in-law had the same frightening experience on the common. She described the monster they saw as 'A phantom dog the size of a calf', adding that on stormy nights it had often been seen and heard in its travel between Aldeburgh and Cromer, and that the marks of its claws were visible on Bungay Church and Blythburgh Church.

MacGregor also collected another story from the same locality which he committed to paper.

As recently as 1953, a widow lady, middle-aged, living on Walberswick Common, not far from the old railway station, was walking with her little dog in the moonlight up Squire's Hill, a small rise near her cottage, when she suddenly noticed a man standing at the top of the hill. On getting closer to him, he vanished. Looking downhill and everywhere about her, she could see him nowhere, nor hear the faintest noise of his movement. The dog refused to accompany her farther, and made for home, shivering with apprehension. She is certain she saw somebody's ghost. Was it that of Sir Ralph Blois, the wealthy miser who owned all that land, who died only a few years ago, and is still earth-bound? If so, it would be wearing his old, white, flannel trousers!

Discussing this account in Walberswick – in particular the extraordinary Sir Ralph – gained me another eerie story about a converted farmhouse that had once belonged to a miser. Apparently this building, close to the village's other popular hostelry, the Bell Inn, had been subjected for years to the sound of rappings on the floor, the occasional groans, and sometimes the sight of an old man near one of the fireplaces who appeared to be gripped by convulsions.

There was, however, a likely solution to the haunting, I was informed. The farmhouse had originally been part of Valley Farm, a section of Sir Ralph's estate, and for close on two hundred years had been let to a family named Goddard. Many of the men had, it seemed, been driven to suicide and their womenfolk committed to the asylum – giving the place the reputation of being a most unhappy house.

At the picturesque Bell Inn which I naturally visited, another story was added to my collection. Back in the smuggling days a coastguard was said to have been returning home from the beach when he saw something strange in the dawn light close to the pub. Being armed – as all officers of His Majesty were in those lawless days for protection against the dangerous smugglers – he took out his pistol and shouted. When the 'evil thing', as the man was later to call it, failed to stop and crossed the road in front of him, he opened fire. Though he was sure he hit the phantom, it disappeared in an instant leaving no trace of its passing whatsoever.

A short walk from the Bell stands Walberswick parish church with it magnificent tower – which has been described as one of the four best towers in Suffolk. The church also has a ghost that has been seen several times by members of the congregation. Most recently, a phantom who appears to be a gentleman in Victorian clothes with what looks like a roll of paper under his arm, was seen by a group of choristers at practice. One theory has it that the man may be the spirit of a former church-warden.

A far more sinister figure is 'Black Toby' who several local people assured me was Walberswick's most famous spectre. Certainly he is the only one of all those I have mentioned to earn an entry in the *Reader's Digest Book of Folklore, Myth and Legends of Britain* (1973).

The ghost is a rare spirit indeed, for he is said to be a Negro drummer who murdered a local girl and is now condemned to eternal punishment as a wandering ghost. His story makes fascinating reading.

In the year 1750 a young girl from Walberswick was found brutally murdered at a place called The Walks, about a mile from the village on the way to Westleton, a small inland community. It seemed that the girl had been on her way to a lover's tryst when she had been attacked and brutally murdered. A hunt for the killer was quickly organized and suspicion fell almost at once on Thomas Gill, a black drummer from a regiment of dragoons, then stationed in the neighbourhood.

Gill was arrested, summarily tried and found guilty. He was sentenced to be hanged from a tree at the scene of his crime. Since that date the place has become known as 'Toby's Walk' and there have been stories of a black ghost seen in the vicinity a number of times. But the dragoon is not beating his drum like the spectre in that famous story of a phantom drummer in the Ingoldsby Legends. As the *Reader's Digest* book colourfully explains:

Ever since the hanging, Walberswick tradition has maintained that a phantom coach occasionally careers down the lane, its headless horse whipped on by a phantom Negro coachman.

Also on the outskirts of Walberswick is another curious spot known as 'Dead Man's Gully' which is similarly said to be haunted. Unlike the grim and rather forbidding aspect of 'Toby's Walk', however, this locality proves, rather disappointingly, to be an abandoned railway line.

Years ago, it seems, Walberswick was joined to Blythburgh not just by a road (today designated the B1387) but also a steam railway service. This had been a natural development for a then important town with a bustling quayside on the River Blythe, much used by merchants involved in the Suffolk wool trade. But with the growth of the size of ships and the harbour suffering the same silting that had swamped Walberswick, Blythburgh in time shrunk to the small community it is today. Indeed, all that remains of its grandeur is the splendid fifteenth century church of Holy Trinity which is widely known as the Cathedral of the Marshes.

Although the railway tracks between the two villages have long since been removed, the strip of embankment they ran along makes a good footpath and passes underneath a bridge which also serves to remind strollers of the walk's original purpose. But this said, there is no mention on any map of this abandoned line of a spot called 'Dead Man's Gully'. So how did it get its name – and its reputation for being a haunt of the 'Whisperers'?

It was in the early sixties that some riders from Walberswick first reported there was something strange about the place when their horses shied up and refused to be ridden along the track. Other reports followed of a strange, moaning sound heard by several different people taking the same walk – and they said the noises were as likely to be heard by day as night. Then, conclusively it seemed, a misty figure that appeared to be appealing for help was observed by a terrified couple near the railway arch.

Though there is no record of any deaths on the railway line during its years of operation, I was told that there is a local belief that the track was laid over what may have been an old burial ground, possibly Viking. Could this have been the origin of the sinister haunting? Though it might partly explain the use of the name 'Dead Man's Gully', further than that it emphasizes the strange nature of the event.

After I had walked along the line to Blythburgh and back – without sight or sound of anything untoward – I returned to the Anchor Inn where I had begun my enquiries to confirm the story of a haunting there which was claimed to have inspired a famous ghost story most people believe to be wholly fictitious.

The Anchor, although built in 1923, actually replaced a much older inn of the same name which had stood on a plot about fifty yards away until it was demolished in the early 1920's. The old Anchor had apparently been much frequented by smugglers in its day, and when it was being pulled down a bricked-up door in the cellar leading to a secret passageway was uncovered.

The Winyard family who had lived in the old pub for the last fifty odd years before its demolition are still well remembered in the area – as are their stories of the strange rustling noises that often disturbed their sleep around midnight. Nor was that all. For these sounds were more often than not accompanied by the bedclothes being snatched from their beds and hurled to the floor by unseen hands. The unusual nature of this haunting – which has not been repeated in the new Anchor according to its present occupants – has led to claims that it was the inspiration for a famous supernatural story, *Oh, Whistle, And I'll Come To You, My Lad* written in 1904 by M.R. James, the famous ghost story writer who was born and brought up in East Anglia.

James was apparently a frequent visitor to this coast, and there seems little doubt he heard all about the legend of the 'Walberswick Whisperers'. Indeed, I believe the evidence is plain to see in his story, in which Walberswick is thinly disguised as Burnstow and a central part of the 'soopy-natural' element concerns some animated bedclothes.

The story, for those who have not read it, concerns a university scholar named Professor Parkin with a passionate interest in antiquities. (He might well be James, in fact, for the author himself was a great student of antiquities while at King's College and Eton.) In any event, Parkins comes to Burnstow to relax, explore the dunes and play some golf. (Shades here of Sir Arthur Conan Doyle at Cromer!) In order to do so, he books himself a large, double-bedded room overlooking the sea in the Globe Inn, an old tavern much associated with smuggling which is believed to be haunted.

Not long after his arrival, while he is out walking on the beach, Parkins discovers an ancient metal whistle in the sand which he takes back to his room. That night, after cleaning it and uncovering a curious Latin inscription, 'Who is this who is coming?', he decides to find out by blowing the instrument. In the pages of the story which follow the startled antiquitarian learns that the curious whining sound emitted by it summons up a 'Walberswick Whistler' in the form of a terrific gust of wind which moans and rattles around the hotel.

Another result of playing the whistle is that the professor begins to have visions of a man scrambling desperately across the groynes of a beach, apparently trying to escape from something terrible. The beach is one which Parkins recognizes immediately as the self-same one he can see outside his window. Let me now quote a couple of relevant sections from this story as it builds to its chilling finale:

So far no cause whatever for the fear of the runner had been shown; but now there began to be seen, far up the shore, a little flicker of something light-coloured moving to and fro with great swiftness and irregularity. Rapidly growing larger, it, too, declared itself as a figure in pale, fluttering draperies, ill-defined. There was something about its motion which made Parkins very unwilling to see it at close quarters. It would stop, raise arms, bow itself toward the sand, then run stooping across the beach to the water-edge and back again; and then, rising upright, once more continue its course forward at a speed that was startling and terrifying.

Just before the figure reaches the exhausted runner on the beach, however, the professor awakens in panic and can sleep no more. In the morning, he is horrified to discover that the second bed in his room bears the unmistakable signs of having been slept in during the night: the sheets crumpled and thrown about. Indeed, on subsequent days no matter how often the bed is remade, whenever Parkins vacates the room for any period of time he returns to find it once more in disarray.

Though the professor spends each day vainly searching for clues to the meaning of his strange vision, every night his sleep is disturbed by the eerie figure moving ever closer along the beach. Then comes the terrible night when Parkins awakens to find something actually stirring in the bed next to his own. As he leaps up, he sees a figure also begin to get out of the other bed.

> It stood for a moment in a band of dark shadow, and he had not seen what its face was like. Now it began to move, in a stooping posture, and all at once the spectator realised, with some horror and some relief, that it must be blind, for it seemed to feel about it with its muffled arms in a groping and random fashion. Turning half way from him, it became suddenly conscious of the bed he had just left, and darted towards it, and bent over the pillows in a way which made Parkins shudder as he had never in his life thought it possible. In a very few moments it seemed to know that the bed was empty, and then, moving forward into the area of light and facing the window, it showed for the first time what manner of thing it was.
>
> Parkins, who very much dislikes being questioned about it, did once describe something of it in my hearing, and I gathered that what he chiefly remembers about it is a horrible, an intensely horrible, face of crumpled linen.

At this, the professor lets out a terrible cry and sinks, fainting, to the floor. Hearing this, another guest and a couple of members of the hotel staff burst into his room where they find the academic sprawled beside a tumbled heap of bedclothes. M.R. James concludes his dramatic story with these words:

> Exactly what explanation was patched up for the staff and visitors at the hotel I must confess I do not recollect. The Professor was somehow cleared of the ready suspicion of

delirium tremens, and the hotel of the reputation of a troubled house.

So ends *Oh, Whistle, And I'll Come To You My Lad*, and I have been interested to learn that a number of other writers share my opinion that the story is influenced by the legend of the 'Walberswick Whiperers'. Amongst these is the highly regarded travel writer, Norman Shrapnel, who recently wrote an essay *A Seaside Haunt* about this particular stretch of coastline which he calls 'the spookiest place in England'.

> Here are M.R. James' groynes, barriers of blackened wood running down to the water over which, as over hurdles in some diabolical race, one of his characters clambers in exhausted terror. He has seen something particularly nasty on the shore. And nobody who has read James can walk along that particular beach without turning his head at least once, thinking he sees 'the shape of a rather indistinct personage in the distance', who seems to be making great efforts to catch him up...

This, however, is not quite the end of my story about the 'Walberswick Whispers', for a suggestion was made to me while I was writing this book. If true, then these ghostly phenomena may be spreading further afield, beyond the confines of Walberswick and Southwold, to the north towards Lowestoft. For at Worlingham, a picturesque and quiet little village close to the famous fishing port, a number of local people have reported an unearthly whining sound that has defied any explanation other than being caused by the supernatural.

The noise, which has been heard mostly at night though also occasionally on wild and stormy days, was at first believed to be caused by a generator or pumping equipment, but these claims were subsequently investigated by local council officials and firmly dismissed. Then a new twist was given to the mystery when it became evident that virtually every instance of the noise has been reported by a woman.

One lady who has frequently heard the sound is a pensioner, Mrs May Moore who lives on the Lowestoft road. She said recently, 'I've been hearing the noise on and off for some years now and at first I thought I was going batty until I learned that other people were hearing it, too. It's a low-key, pulsating noise which seems to go right through you. It's worst at night and there is no way to shut it out of your head.'

Although neither Mrs Moore – nor any of the officials of the local electricity, gas or water companies who have also come under suspicion and similarly investigated the mystery – can offer any solution, I did meet one long time resident of Worlingham who was prepared to offer a suggestion. He asked, though, that I did not disclose his name.

'Now folks say animals can hear things that us humans can't,' he confided. 'Well, I reckon there are some supernatural things that only women are sensitive to. That's what this noise could be. If it ain't that, then it has to be one of them 'Walberswick Whispers'.'

I was quite taken aback at this suggestion for I had made no mention of the phenomena while enquiring about the mysterious sounds in Worlingham. But I couldn't help thinking back to the story of 'Dead Man's Gully' and the horses that had shied away from that haunted locality.

'So you know about the 'Walberswick Whistlers'?' I asked my informant.

'Course I do,' came the reply. 'Everyone on this coast does. They ain't your ordinary sort of ghosts. Make all sorts of funny noises. You go to Walberswick and ask them there. They'll tell you.'

I somehow couldn't bring myself to tell my helpful friend that I had already done so. For whether his assumption was true or not, what he had unwittingly done was confirm the enduring belief in the existence of the phenomena in this part of East Anglia. For myself, ever since that day I have been quite unable to listen to the sound of the wind moaning around any hotel or house without being reminded of the strange stories of the 'Walberswick Whistlers'....

# 6   The Lost World of Dunwich

The cluster of small homes and fishermen's cottages which form the little community of Dunwich on the Suffolk coast provide an entrance way to a unique world where the living daily mix with the dead. For here in the aptly named Sole Bay lie the submerged ruins of what was once one of the most prosperous ports in England. Its doom, it is said, is still being tolled by the occasional muffled chiming of underwater bells that many a local person claims to have heard over the years...

The juxtaposition of the ancient and modern is perhaps nowhere else more vividly demonstrated on the East Anglian coast than at this particular spot. Legend tell us of a mighty storm centuries ago which devastated one of the jewels of the entire coast – while today the awesome presence of the Sizewell Atomic Power Station is clearly visible less than four miles away across the wetlands of Minsmere. And just as the Roman legions once established a military fort here, so, during World War II, was the second radar station in England – indeed, in the entire world. It was sited on Dunwich Heath as an early warning system against the 'Doodlebugs': the German V-1 flying bombs which were to prove the forerunners of today's space rockets.

The visitor to this windswept and stark stretch of coastland may, initially, be surprised at the lack of evidence of a flourishing community having once existed here. Soon, though, he comes to sense a strange atmosphere about the place which some have referred to as a mixture of the secret and the magical which excites the

79

senses. The visitor also comes to appreciate that what makes it so eerie is the very fact that there is so little evidence.

The feeling that there is something magical about Dunwich has been perhaps most aptly put by the historian W.A. Dutt in his book *Highways and Byways of East Anglia*. 'Like the tales of lost Atlantis and the mythical land of Lyonesse, the story of Dunwich seizes upon the imagination,' he writes, 'though when one sees how little remains of what may once have been the chief city of East Anglia, it is difficult to believe that Dunwich, too, was not a phantom city of a land of dreams.'

This association of Dunwich with the supernatural has, if anything, been put even more vividly by a writer from the *Daily Mail*, who after a visit a couple of years ago described it quite simply as 'the eeriest place in the British Isles where the chimes of sunken bells summon the ghosts of a lost world.'

It becomes evident almost at once to the visitor that what remaining signs there are of the lost city perch on a few yards of land on the edge of crumbling, sandy cliffs directly facing the sea. It is clear too that these precarious remnants have survived simply because they were built outside the old city walls.

Strolling along the present St James Street out from the village, a walker will find himself led directly to the cliff edge over what was quite obviously a main road leading into the very heart of old Dunwich. A second road, Middle Street, also once served the southern part of the town, but today cuts a path through a curiously silent wood until it, too, disappears spectacularly over the cliff.

The remnants of what must have been two fine buildings, however, survived the ravages of the elements: a flint wall and archway around the site of Greyfriars Priory; and part of the chapel of a twelfth century leper colony, which was, of necessity, built well outside the city.

There are stories that this area is haunted and certainly to visit the place as evening is falling – or even more so on a wild winter's night when the incoming tide is once again lashing at the cliffs – makes it easy to understand why.

According to local gossip, shadowy figures have been seen on the cliff top for the past hundred years and more and are believed to be the ghosts of Dunwich's former citizens.

Mysterious lights in the ruins of the priory have likewise been reported on several occasions by present residents, as well as strange sounds which are said to be uncannily like the chanting of monks. These tales have been investigated by a number of experts, including Alistair Alpin MacGregor who, after a visit in 1955, substantiated the claims in an article for *Country Life*.

> There seems no doubt that the ruins of Greyfriars, the old monastery at Dunwich, is haunted, its long, grey wall still well preserved, still eloquent in their desertion and decay. The ghosts of monks are seen, silently treading its precincts; and folks there are in the neighbourhood who swear that they have observed ghostly lights dimly glowing among the ruins, and heard not only phantom bells, but also phantom voices, intoning some ancient Franciscan versicle.

In his article, Mr MacGregor added an intriguing footnote.

> Dunwich is rumoured to have at least one other ghost – that of an Elizabethan dressed in the stylish clothes of that period who is seen walking down toward the sea and taking a boat. Could he be a lost soul from the old city endeavouring to return home? I would be glad to hear from any reader who knows about this ancient phantom.

So, too, would the writer of this book. For my own enquiries about this remarkable phantom produced no new evidence and only the suggestion that the Elizabethan had been seen again just once since the fifties by a lady who subsequently left East Anglia.

It is on the very edge of the cliffs at Dunwich that most visitors pause to look out over the grey, rolling turmoil of the North Sea, and it is here that the most poignant reminder of the lost world is to be found. A tilted, weatherbeaten gravestone bears the almost cruelly appropriate name, John Brinkley Easey, who has lain on the 'brink' here, anything but 'easily' since 1826!

This headstone is the only visible trace of the graveyard of the huge church of All Saints' which, piece by piece – first the chancel, then the nave and finally the tower – succumbed to the inexorable pounding of the sea, finally disappearing into the waves in 1919. Perhaps not the only trace … because according to local people there are still many other unmarked graves in the 255 ft long graveyard, from which the constant erosion is continuing to release bones into the sea with every passing year.

Indeed, quite a number of visitors in recent years have been shocked to find parts of skeletons and even the occasional skull lying on the exposed cliff's edge after a particularly high tide or very stormy night. In the fullness of time, of course, the last remains of John Brinkley Easey will also inevitably suffer this same fate…

It seems more than likely that some of these unearthed bones may have belonged to men and women who lived when Dunwich was a city complete with its own cathedral and churches, schools and inns, houses and farms, and bore all the signs of being a well populated, busy seaport. Researchers believe that as the sea encroached upon Dunwich, the wealthier and more influential families moved their dead further inland, the last of these reinterments taking place at All Saints'.

Though such a conclusion is obviously open to dispute, there can be no argument about the existence of a number of ruins lying just beneath the waves, for these have been located recently by divers and confirm the validity of the legend. But it was not primarily the ruins of the vanished city that brought me to Dunwich, but the stories of the supernatural underwater bells. Nor did my search end there, for the visit also provided me with the first clue towards solving another famous Suffolk legend, the mystery of the 'Green Children of Woolpit.' But of that, more later.

The history of Dunwich can be summarized with reasonable authority from a number of existing documents and records. Although other towns and villages along this coast have been lost, this was undoubtedly the most important community to have fallen victim to the ravages of Neptune's waves.

The earliest inhabitants of the lost landmass were probably ancient Britons, whose priests, the Druids, had a magical association with both man and nature. Then came the invading Romans with their military station which some historians believe may have been given the romantic sounding title of Sitomagus. The fifth century saw the arrival of the Saxons – in particular the Angles – who gave their name to this portion of the British Isles. They, in fact, named the place Dunmoc (the Anglo-Saxon for Dunwich) and in a matter of a few years the presence of the Saxon East Anglian Royal House turned the flourishing locality into its capital city.

In the century which followed Dunwich continued to grow in size, and under the Normans reached its peak of importance and influence. By the reign of Henry II, records indicate that the city boasted a king's palace, a bishop's seat, a money mint, several hospitals, fifty-two places of worship, numerous markets, a vibrant fishing and ship building industry, and row upon row of houses for the 5,000 citizens and merchants. All of this was surrounded by a protective wall with huge and richly embellished bronze gates.

The people of Dunwich were, however, well aware of the power of the North Sea which occasionally pounded at their stronghold, and erosion was kept at bay by piling brushwood, weighted with stones, on the shingle. This task was carried out each autumn and for centuries proved to be quite satisfactory to give protection for the ensuing winter.

Sufficient protection, that is, until one calamitous night in January 1326. In less than six hours a terrible storm raged about Dunwich, destroying over 400 homes and buildings, and banking over one million tons of sand and shingle across the harbour mouth, cutting it off from the sea and thereby making it useless as a port.

As a result of that terrible night Dunwich was doomed. Although the authorities tried vainly to reopen the port, first the fishermen and then the merchants began to drift away to other more suitable locations. Despite financial aid from several subsequent monarchs including Queen Elizabeth I and King James II the sea continued to eat away at the land and as it did more residents still left for Southwold, Ipswich and even beyond. The once glorious port was now left at the mercy of the elements and by the early years of the eighteenth century many important buildings including the town hall, numerous churches and several rows of buildings had disappeared forever under the sea. In 1832, Dunwich's last major sign of importance was removed when it lost its parliamentary seat.

In the years which have followed, the sea has virtually finished its work of obliterating Dunwich from the map of England, leaving only the small community huddled behind the shallow cliff – which today's visitors find by turning off from the A12 at Yoxford. But if the city itself has gone, the romance surrounding its name lives on – aided by the stories of the phantom bells.

A visitor does not need to search too long to find someone on this stretch of coast who has heard the bells ringing out above the pounding of the waves. Curiously, it is said that the complete octave is never heard as one of the bells in the peel always remains silent.

Usually the chimes are heard at night, but occasionally during the day. They have been particularly noted in July and November when two of old Dunwich's great annual fairs, those of St James and St Leonard, were held. Sometimes they have been heard at Christmas, too, when local folk say they are warning of stormy weather at sea.

Elliott O'Donnell, the famous ghost hunter who wrote dozens of books about curious supernatural phenomena and investigated a number of stories of phantom bells, had this to say about the Dunwich peel in his book, *Strange Sea Mysteries* (1939):

In the little Suffolk coastal village of Dunwich there are people who hear not only the lowing of herds on drowned pastures and the clippity-clop of shod hooves on ancient streets, but also the chiming of phantom bells wafting inland. They recognise the chiming readily because of the missing note. When several of the inhabitants of this neighbourhood claim to have heard these bells, it is customary to make enquiries over a fairly large area so as to ascertain whether, by any chance, the bells of some known church happened to be ringing at that time. Invariably it is found that no such bells were – and in any case, the ghost bells are usually heard at an hour of the night when no human being would be active in a church belfry.

My main informant about the underwater bells was Tom Marten, a born and bred Suffolk man who lives in Theberton, a couple of miles from Dunwich. This doughty old salt who has fished around the East Anglian coast all his life told me that 'A lot of folk I know have heard those bells ringing under the sea. A sort of muffled, distorted sound they make, as if they were still in their steeples.

'They say that in ancient times when the sea destroyed Dunwich, the church in its turn cursed the sea. Nowadays, though, the vicar blesses the sea each year so that it won't wear any more of the cliffs down or be too rough for the fishing boats.'

Tom pauses and grins to himself as another story associated with the bells slips into his mind. 'There's one old tale reckons they are being rung by a mermaid who wants to lure sailors' and fishermens' boats onto the rocks,' he says. 'More likely story is that they are ringing out a warning of an approaching storm,' he added.

As if to add more weight to his opinion, Tom showed me a copy of a well-thumbed paperback volume he had in his possession entitled *Bogie Tales of East Anglia* by M.H. James, published locally in Ipswich in 1891. For one moment as he passed over the book I thought I had come across an unknown collection by the great ghost story writer, M.R. James, and I could not help feeling rather disappointed when a closer look at the author's second initial convinced me it was not the same person. In fact, on reading the preface the writer turned out to be a lady. But what this local Victorian gentlewoman had to say about the Dunwich tradition none the less made fascinating reading.

> The sea, warringly ceaselessly with the land at this part of the coast, encroaches yearly, devouring shore and sand-cliff; at another part, slowly receding, it casts up sandy spits and alters the configuration of the shore. In older days these encroachments were more sudden, and once the greater part of the town was thus swept away, its streets and its churches submerged. Fishermen will tell you that on still nights, when they lie out in their boats, in the bay, after the fat 'longshore herring', the bells of the old churches chime clear and sweet below the ripples, and one who had a fine imagination is said to claim to have seen, one very low tide, the walls of houses and buildings!

While one hundred years ago Miss James may have metaphorically raised her eyebrows at this suggestion, recent diving activities off the coast of Dunwich have substantiated every word of those fishermens' claims. Among those divers who have braved the dark and turbulent waves of the North Sea to try to find the ruins of the lost world is a marine archaeologist and experienced subaqua diver named Stuart Bacon who told me about his discoveries.

Stuart remembers first visiting Dunwich as a child when he used to spend hours sitting on the last remaining ruins of All Saints' Church at the sea's edge wondering exactly what lay beneath the waves. Then, as an adult, he began to answer these questions in 1971 with the help of divers from the North-East Essex Subaqua Club.

It is a fact that the North Sea is not a good diving area – underwater visibility only extends to a maximum of 20 ft when the conditions are perfect. Mostly the divers have to work by touch in almost total blackness and there are usually strong currents to contend with. Despite this the group were not long in finding the ruins of All Saints' Church quite close to the shore. During his dives, Stuart found that the ruins were now the home of a mass of colourful sea life.

Almost two years later, the club members located the ruins of another church, St Peter's, approximately a quarter of a mile from the shore and about 35 ft below the surface. It, too, is now in the process of being mapped and measured by the divers.

It was when St Peter's was first discovered that the old legend of the underwater bells of Dunwich took on a whole new meaning for Stuart Bacon. He explains his own change of attitude to what he now refers to as 'the ghostly city' in these words.

'Many people believe Dunwich to be haunted', he says, 'and a number of divers have reported a strange presence or odd feeling, especially if conditions are black. The diver who first discovered St Peter's church recorded in his log that he felt "very elated" at the location of the ruins, but he was "aware of the presence of something or someone beside me". But there was, though, no other diver in the sea at Dunwich that day.'

This strange experience made Stuart determined to find out if there might be any truth in the stories about subterranean bells being rung by unseen hands.

'The legendary bells of Dunwich which some people say they have heard to this day, either from the cliff top or at the change of tide on the beach and normally at midnight, are regarded as complete rubbish by a lot of "straight thinking" people,' he says. 'However, once you get underwater and among the ruins of All Saints', and catch sight of part of the tower on its side, the legend rapidly takes on quite a different aspect – and a glimpse of the ruins of St Peter's which stood on the cliff edge 300 years ago can be persuasive even to a cynical marine archaeologist like myself!'

Stuart begins to really warm to his theme. 'But, of course, there could be no ringing of bells from the last three churches to tumble down the cliffs as we know the bells were removed long before the churches were lost. The legend must therefore originate from one or more of the other seven lost churches which have been recorded. And as we have no records of the whereabouts of all their bells, it is feasible that some of them could still be out there beneath the waves.'

The members of the Subaqua Club have every intention of continuing their research into the lost world of Dunwich, and though Stuart Bacon himself has yet to hear the ghostly bells he does not now dismiss claims by others to have heard them. Indeed, along with local historians, he is anxious to log any reports of them – for he is convinced that Dunwich still has many of its secrets to reveal...

Quite by chance, as I was nearing the end of my research in Dunwich, I came across another reference about the lost city which offered a possible explanation for a quite different Suffolk mystery that had engaged my attention, off and on, for some time. This is the legend of the 'Green Children of Woolpit.' Why I should have made the connection I am not really sure to this day. But as it may just provide a solution to a 700 year old riddle as to just where those strange infants really came from, I should like to include it here.

The reference which caught my eye was contained in a little work entitled *Historical Notes on Dunwich, Blythburgh and Southwold*, written by a local authority, T. Gardner. In his book he noted that in the year 1216, a group of ships carrying some 40,000 Flemings sailed from France to settle in Norfolk and Suffolk. The destination of the ships was, naturally enough, the famous seaport of Dunwich. However, just before they reached the harbour, a terrible storm apparently blew up and virtually all the ships and their passengers – men, women and children – were swept away to their deaths. Only a few pathetic survivors made it to the shore, the report added.

It was the date of 1216 that caught my eye. For I knew from my study of the story of the green children that that was the year, according to most accounts, when the pair of children with their sallow skin – described as green in a contemporary report – had first been seen. The youngsters, who could not speak a word of English, had dramatically appeared in the little village of Woolpit, four miles from the important city of Bury St Edmunds.

Woolpit, I knew from my study of maps of East Anglia,

was situated thirty miles directly west of Dunwich. In the countryside between Dunwich and Woolpit at that time there were no more than a few scattered rural villages and not a single major town.

Could those two children, I wondered as I read the reference, have been among the survivors of the storm? And when they found themselves washed up on a strange shore with no sign of their loved ones, could they have set off to try and find them? And in so doing could they have stumbled into Woolpit ... and thereafter into legend?

Excited by these thoughts, I again looked up the only contemporary account of the green children and decided to drive the short distance from the coast to Woolpit to test my idea...

The story of the children was first recorded in Latin by a native of Cambridgeshire, Ralph de Coggeshall, who was for twenty years the abbot of a Cistercian monastery until about 1225. An English translation by J. Stevenson tells the tale in colourful detail.

A wonderful thing happened in Suffolk, at St Mary's of the Wolf-pits (the original name of Woolpit). A boy and his sister were found by the inhabitants of that place near the mouth of a pit which is there, who had the form of all their limbs like to those of other men, but they differed in the colour of their skin from our people, for the whole surface of their skin was tinged of a colour green. No one could understand their speech. When they were brought as curiosities to the house of a certain knight, Sir Richard de Calne, they wept bitterly. Bread and other victuals were set before them, but they would touch none of them, though they were tormented by great hunger.

At length, when some beans just cut, with their stalks, were brought into the house, they made signs, with great avidity, that they should be given to them. When they were brought, they opened the stalks instead of the pods, thinking the beans were in the hollow of them; but not finding them there, they began to weep anew. When those present saw this, they opened the pods and showed them the naked beans. They fed on these with great delight, and for a long time tasted no other food.

Then gradually their colour changed as the nature of the
food changed them and they lost completely their green
colour. The boy, however, was always languid and
depressed, and he died within a short time. The girl
enjoyed continual good health; and lived for some years in
the service of that knight. Afterwards she became like
other women and later married a man from King's Lynn.

The story of these strange children has naturally been
much debated and analyzed over the intervening
centuries, as well as bringing curiosity seekers to Woolpit,
where the remaining pits are now neatly bisected by the
A45 road from Ipwich to Bury St Edmunds. Although it is
possible to look over these pits, from which vast quantities
of gravel have been extracted, it is quite impossible to
determine in which one the children were found.

The theories which have been advanced for the origin of
the children are various. One of the earliest suggested
they had come from an underground world, hence their
green skin; another that they had been abandoned and
raised by animals, perhaps wolves. More recently, it has
been argued firstly that they could have been 'teleported'
from another dimension; secondly, that they might have
been aliens from another planet who had become
separated from their spacecraft; and, thirdly, that they
were from the lost world of Atlantis. There are also, of
course, those writers who are convinced the story is pure
fable from start to finish.

My belief, however, having examined all the evidence
again, is that it is far more likely that they came from the
lost world of Dunwich, two survivors from that party of
Flemings shipwrecked off the Suffolk coast. The sallow,
almost olive colouring of the Flemish people could easily
have been confused by the much darker Suffolk folk as
being green, and the language they spoke would
obviously have been unintelligible to the simple country
people of the time.

At least two other people who have written about the
green children believe there is a more commonplace
explanation for their origin than underground worlds or

spaceships. Grace Pickthall who published an interesting article on the topic in the *East Anglian Magazine* in March 1957 said that any suggestion they might not have been human could be discounted by the fact that, 'the girl grew up and had several children, both boys and girls, and until comparatively recent days – the early 1900's – some descendents of theirs were still living in King's Lynn.' None of these descendents had green skin and all were perfectly normal in every way, she added.

This view is also shared by Mr V.A. Jones who lives at Elmwell, a small village on the other side of the A45, which is believed to be the locality of Sir Richard de Calne's house. He, too, has carried out extensive investigations into the story and told me that he had actually been visited by a man who claimed he was related to the brother and sister.

'Although it is a fascinating mystery, the answer to where they came from is much more likely to be in Europe, possibly Scandinavia,' he says, 'though how they got to Woolpit is the biggest puzzle of all. They must have crossed the North Sea somewhere. The port of Ipswich which was also open at that time is another possibility.'

Like the ringing of the subterranean bells of Dunwich, the mystery of the 'Green Children of Woolpit' will doubtless continue to excite controversy. Although I cannot substantiate my idea of the association between the two any more definitely than any of the other theories, it is surely very much in keeping with all the intriguing possibilities which give the 'supernatural coast' of East Anglia its unique fascination.

# 7 The Devil's Skull in Woodbridge

Woodbridge is one of the most attractive small towns to be found along the Suffolk coast, despite the fact that it is only a matter of a few miles from the two big ports of Felixstowe and Harwich which are forever busy with shipping to and from the continent. The town's name was actually derived from the Anglo-Saxon 'Woden Burh', which means 'Woden's Town', and is striking evidence that this was an important locality as early as Saxon times. The foreshore with its boatyards and chandleries is further proof that the place has provided ideal harbouring from the ebb and flow of the strong North Sea tides for many years.

Yet this picturesque community with its magnificent Dutch-gabled Shire Hall and superb eighteenth century weather-boarded Tide Mill is also the centre of an intriguing mystery – in fact, two mysteries, both concerning one of the most enigmatic figures of British history, Oliver Cromwell. The first of these relates to a skull believed to be that of the Lord Protector of England which belonged to a local clergyman, Canon Horace Wilkinson of Melton Grove; and the second is a remarkable legend that Cromwell was actually a practicing satanist who had made a pact wih the devil in order to secure control of England.

This skull had apparently been severed from Cromwell's body after the removal of his corpse from Westminster Abbey following the Restoration of the Stuart monarchy. Thereafter it had passed in some secrecy through various hands until it finally came to light in Woodbridge earlier this century. The story of the protector's association with devil worship is said to have its origin in events which occurred during the closing years of his life.

It seems somehow appropriate that the skull should have resurfaced again at Woodbridge – for it was close by at Sutton Hoo that an equally gruesome-looking relic was unearthed in 1939. This was a bronze and iron helmet looking very like a crude representation of a skull which turned out to be part of a hoard of buried treasure belonging to a Saxon king who had been interred in his sea-going ship in a huge pit. The treasure, which included priceless coins, jewellery and oher regalia, is now in the British Museum and experts believe it may well have belonged to King Raedwald, the King of East Anglia from about AD 610 to 625. But this fact has never been established beyond question because no trace of a body was ever found amidst all the treasure...

But to return to the mysteries of Cromwell's skull and his dealings with the devil. The first person to bring the Woodbridge association to widespread public attention was a BBC radio broadcaster named John Keir Cross in a programme he transmitted at Hallowe'en in 1953. Cross was a phlegmatic Scotsman who had made his reputation as an adapter of radio dramas in the years immediately after the Second World War. His Scots ancestry also gave him an abiding interest in the supernatural, and among his books can be found several outstanding collections of occult tales including *The Other Passenger* and *Black Magic Stories*.

It was while John was collecting items for his Hallowe'en broadcast that he came across references to the legend of Cromwell having dabbled in black magic and the story that the protector's skull was believed to have survived the ravages of time and was now in the possession of a Canon Wilkinson in Woodbridge. He subsequently met the canon, was shown the grisly skull kept carefully wrapped in red and black silk in a large oak box, and revealed the facts in his broadcast. One result of the programme was a most unnerving experience for him which seemed to add emphasis to the legend: the other was the stimulation of further investigation into the story...

The sequence of events preceding the broadcast had begun when Cross had decided to do something a little different for Hallowe'en – the night, of course, when witches and warlocks are traditionally abroad practicing their ancient magic. It was intended to be a general survey of the occult, John explained afterwards, 'in which we set out to explore, among many other things, the uneasy relationship between James VI – who was a devil's advocate without knowing it – and the mysterious 'Black Man of North Berwick'; the self-confessed vampirism of Elizabeth, Countess Bathory; and the curious evidence that Oliver Cromwell might well have been involved in satanic activities.'

As a kind of gimmick to attract listeners, it was also decided to end the programme by drawing a genuine magic circle around the microphone and getting an actor to read out an authentic medieval incantation for summoning the devil. After this, everyone involved with the programme was to leave the studio, switch off the lights, and leave the microphone open for two minutes to see if anything might happen.

Nothing, in fact, did happen in the studio. But later that same night John Keir Cross was himself subjected to a terrifying ordeal in his own flat. As he and his wife sat in their living-room discussing the broadcast, and in particular the anticlimax of the last two minutes, they suddenly heard terrified screams coming from the adjoining bedroom where their 6-month-old son was sleeping. When the couple rushed into the baby's room they were horrified to find him with blood all over his face and hands.

John immediately snatched the screaming child from its cot and dashed into the living-room, slamming the bedroom door behind him. As his wife began to comfort the infant, he rang their doctor. And while the couple sat waiting impatiently for the GP to arrive, both were convinced they heard something scrabbling and gnawing inside the nursery.

As the doctor was dressing the infant's wounds, he ventured the opinion that the boy had probably been attacked by a rat: and, indeed, the following day Cross found an enormous buck rat still in the room, which, with difficulty, he cornered and killed. What puzzled him, though, was just how the creature had got into a room which had neither a window, a fireplace nor any kind of crack in the wall through which it might have gained entry. And, furthermore, why should it have chosen to enter a flat several floors up in an apartment building?

One answer to these questions was offered to John Kier Cross by a fellow writer who was well versed in black magic and the occult, which sent a shiver up his spine and remained fixed in his memory for the rest of his life.

'You know what really happened?' his friend had said. 'That night on the air you invited the devil to come? Well, he *did* – not in the way you might have expected but in a way which would touch you deeply. The rat – poor little devil – was only his instrument...'

The association of this event and the legend of Cromwell and satanism so deeply affected John Kier Cross that it was some years before he could bring himself to talk about the experience. In the meantime, however, he received a number of letters from listeners to the programme who had been fascinated by the story of Cromwell's skull – one in particular catching his attention. It was from a Robert Thurston Hopkins, himself an investigator into the supernatural, who had been following a similar line of enquiry.

Hopkins, a Suffolk man born in Bury St Edmunds, had become well-known in the forties and fifties as a 'ghost hunter' and produced a number of books based on his experiences such as *Adventures With Phantoms* (1947) and *Ghosts Over England* (1953). Thanks to John Kier Cross's introduction, he, too, visited Canon Wilkinson and saw for himself the mysterious skull. Indeed, he wrote a vivid account of this meeting which, curiously, he did not publish during his lifetime, but which has subsequently come into my possession since his death, along with a number of his books and papers. In this account he also links up with the rumours of Cromwell and his pact with the devil...

Before coming to Hopkins' statement, however, it is perhaps necessary to just remind the reader of a few facts concerning Oliver Cromwell's life. Born in 1599 in Huntingdon, he was educated at Cambridge University, embraced puritanism in its most enthusiastic form as a young man, and in 1628 became an MP. At Westminster he first came to public notice during the third of King Charles's stormy Parliaments when he raised his voice against 'romanizing ecclestiastics'. Then, when the Civil War broke out in 1642, he organized local Puritan forces and fought as a captain of a troop of mounted soldiers at the Battle of Edgehill.

Spurred on by a belief in his own destiny, Cromwell formed the invincible Ironsides, and on 3 September 1651 at Worcester, organized the overwhelming victory against the royalist forces which ended the Civil War and effectively put him in control of the country. We shall be returning to the crucial events of this day when considering the legend of the protector's pact with the devil.

Although Cromwell, as ruler of the nation, was able to effect some important changes in both home and foreign policy, his protectorate was in perpetual conflict with both republican resistance and royalist plots and uprisings. In time, the strain of state affairs began to undermine his health, and then the death of his favourite daughter, Lady Elizabeth Claypole in February 1658, prostrated him with grief and cut short his life. He died on 3 September 1658, and without him the style of government which he had developed and sustained soon began to fall apart. Something very unuual also began to occur. The historian C.D.T.Baker-Carr, in his essay, 'Cromwell's Head', published in 1955, explains.

Then began the series of events unparalleled in the history

of this country, events whose strange quality somehow still linger today in that remote, quiet Suffolk town where his skull has rested for so long. His death occurred at 3 p.m., and was followed swiftly by a post-mortem – his adherents were certain that he had been poisoned. One of the physicians who performed the autopsy was George Bate. He has left the following notes on what they found: 'His Body being opened: in the Animal parts the Vessels of the Brain seem to be overcharged; in the Vitals the Lungs a little inflamed; but in the Natural, the source of the distemper appeared; the Spleen, though sound to the eye, being filled with matter like to the Lees of Oyl.' On September 4, the London Gazette of the day, Mercurius Politicus, stated: 'The Physicians and Chirurgeiens appointed by the Order of the Council to embowel and embalme the Body of his late Highness and fill the same with sweet odours, performed their duty.' Both these extracts give us definite proof that Cromwell's brain was removed and that his body was embalmed – two important points in relation to later events.

Following this embalmment, Cromwell's body was buried privately in the chapel of Henry VII at Westminster Abbey. There it remained for three years during the weak and vacillating rule of his son, Richard, until the restoration of the monarchy under Charles II. Then, on the anniversary of the execution of Charles I – 30 January 1661 – a terrible vengeance was visited on the former Lord Protector. His body, together with those of his son-in-law, Henry Ireton, and his lieutenant John Bradshaw, were dug up from their tombs and taken by a rowdy and jeering crowd to the gallows at Tyburn.

Here the public executioner had been ordered to perform the grisly spectacle of beheading all three corpses. According to contemporary accounts, Cromwell's head proved so tough and stubborn that the executioner was unable to entirely sever it. After taking eight swings at it with his axe, it was left to a cavalry soldier to finish off the decapitation with his sword.

The remains of the three bodies were then dumped into a pit at the foot of the gallows, while the heads were fitted onto spikes and carried by the mob through the streets to Westminster. There at Westminster Hall the crowds watched as the three spiked heads were hauled up into the roof and lashed onto the eaves.

Oliver Cromwell's head was apparently placed beween those of his two colleagues – but that is one of the last facts on record about the grisly relic which later went missing from its place on the roof ... and was rarely seen thereafter until it finally found its way to Woodbridge more than two hundred years later.

According to one legend, Cromwell's head fell from the roof during a storm one night, and when a sentry stumbled over it he decided to take it home. When news of the disappearance reached the government there was an uproar – some members fearing the skull might be used as a rallying point for any Puritan forces who might be still active – and an immediate enquiry was launched. Rather than face the wrath of his superiors – and a certain prison sentence – the terrified sentry concealed the head in the chimney of his home and told no-one about it until he was on his death-bed.

In the interim, the mystery of the lost skull inspired the first rumours that its owner had been in league with the devil, and that it could well have been taken away by the 'evil one' himself. For who else could have scaled to the heights of Westminster Hall without being seen – and wasn't Cromwell promised to Satan anyhow, the tongues wagged?

The legend, however, states that the old sentry's daughter became the skull's new owner after his death, and similarly afraid of what discovery might bring from the authorities, she quickly sold it for the best price she could get. For a while the relic was believed to have been in the possession of the Russell family of Cambridgeshire who had intermarried with the Cromwells.

The next time the skull was heard of, stories associating it with the devil had grown apace. The new owner was a man named Sam Russell – not, apparently, a member of the Cambridgeshire family, though he may well have been distantly related – who described himself as an actor. Sam led a profligate life and was always in debt, but from the moment the skull came into his possession it apparenly also began to exert an evil influence on him.

Russell's life was plagued by mishaps: he was attacked and robbed after a rare successful appearance on stage, and then later fell down the steps of the Covent Garden Theatre and cracked his skull. He was unable to get work and became poorer and poorer. People shunned him and in a desperate attempt to change his luck he sold the skull in 1787 to a dealer named James Cox for £118. Cox, in turn, tried to sell his purchase for £500 to a government official, but was turned away by the man who apparently doubted the relic's authenticity.

A syndicate of three London merchants had no such scruples about the skull, however, and offered Cox £300 for it. The three planned to exhibit it in a shop in Old Bond Street but, so the story goes, no sooner had the relic come into their possession than all three died, one after another, quite suddenly and mysteriously.

The wife of the last of this trio was by now understandably convinced that the relic was possessed by evil and sold it, in 1814, to the son of her doctor, one Josiah Henry Wilkinson. Though Wilkinson was a practical man, and not superstitious, he decided against exploiting his purchase in any way and quietly laid it to rest in an iron-bound casket.

For the next century Cromwell's skull was kept hidden from view by the Wilkinson family. Josiah left it to his son, William, an MP for Lambeth, who died in 1865. In turn, his son, Horace, a member of the Stock Exchange, continued the tradition of secrecy until, in 1908, following his death, it passed to Canon Wilkinson of Melton Grove.

Here, too, it might have remained in the secrecy of its box but for John Keir Cross's broadcast and the revival of interest in the stories of Oliver Cromwell and satanism.

Such, then, was the situation when Robert Thurston Hopkins went to visit Canon Wilkinson, and his typewritten report of their meeting offers a fascinating, first-hand account of the genial clergyman and his gruesome possession. This is what Hopkins has to say:

Canon Wilkinson brought out the dark casket which contained Cromwell's head and exposed it for my inspection. The head is not quite perfect as some of the features have disintegrated, but the pike-head is still embedded in the skull. The pike is thrust upwards through the neck and part of the wooden heft is still attached to it.

The head is still massive and challenging with its cavernous eye sockets and a twisted mouth which seems to still exhibit defiance. The hair is also preserved, a dull, coarse, rusty bronze with a straggly beard and moustache. It is said that the beard was grown during Cromwell's last illness and he would not allow a barber to come near him with a razor for fear it might be an assassin employed by his enemies to cut his throat. The famous wart is now marked by a circular hollow above the right eye.

Canon Wilkinson, as I remember him, seemed to belong to a more spacious era than this present harassed one – an era when culture and good fellowship walked arm-in-arm and took a bottle of wine together in some snug tavern or mellow country mansion. He was nearly eighty and poked fun at his friends with a zest for the brighter side of life.

'Some people say I should give the head to the State,' he told me, 'but they occasionally lose their own heads so how can I expect such a cranky lot of people to take care of this one?' He held it high and continued in a sterner voice, 'When the people did own it, they stuck a pike through it.'

The box which holds the skull was on a table beside the Canon's bed. 'The cat used to sleep on the box,' he said, 'but once when I was showing the skull to a friend, she saw it for the first time. She rushed out of the room like steam – and also like steam she evaporated never to return.'

A number of researchers have also called upon Canon Wilkinson in Woodbridge to view the relic. 'I remember one man who came from the United States specially to see it not long ago,' said Mr Wilkinson. 'I had just taken it out of the box when a sudden flash of lightning played across the skull and the room rocked with a fearful clap of thunder. I thought that the roof had been hit and I rushed out into the garden to look at the roof. I found that only the telephone wires on the roof had been damaged and so I returned to assure my guest that he was not in danger. But he was no longer in the room and through the window I just caught a glimpse of him running down my drive as though the Devil was at his heels!'

This story reminded me of the legend that Oliver Cromwell was supposed to have formed a pact with the Devil in return for corporeal power. At the mention of this a frown crossed the Canon's features and he was silent for a minute. 'Certainly there is evidence in Echard's History of England to that effect,' he said, 'but it is a suggestion that I find difficult to accept.' With that Canon Wilkinson replaced the skull in its casket and as he shut the lid I knew the subject, too, was closed.

There, enigmatically, Robert Thurston Hopkins ended his report on Cromwell's head in Woodbridge. A few years later, Canon Wilkinson died, and on his death the skull was moved once again – to where, I shall disclose shortly. But its departure from Woodbridge has not halted the speculation among some of the residents about its alleged evil influence.

A man who came to investigate these stories was James Wentworth Day, also well-known as an expert on the supernatural in East Anglia. He was something of an authority on Cromwell's local associations, too, which gave him an added interest in the events which were told to him in 1972, just after he had written a special article about Cromwell for the *East Anglian Magazine*.

One old resident wrote to me that there had been reports of a 'ghostly presence' in the vicinity of Melton Grove, and there was even a story that some people walking home one night had heard a kind of moaning, anguished voice in the same place. They said that it sounded just like a person searching for something they had lost. Could it have been the ghost of Oliver Cromwell looking for his missing head, I wondered? – but there was no one who could answer my question.

Tom Wilson, a lifelong resident of Woodbridge, to whom I put the same question was also unable to provide an answer, although he did tell me, 'A lot of folks about here were mighty happy when they heard that the 'Devil's

Head' had left Woodbridge. And even happier when they were told that it had been buried at last in Cambridge.'

In fact, after another period of silence as to the skull's whereabouts after the death of Canon Wilkinson, it was secured by the trustees of Sidney Sussex College at Cambridge – where Oliver Cromwell had been a student – and laid to rest in the college chapel. As to the whereabouts of the rest of Cromwell's body after the decapitation at Tyburn, there are conflicting reports. Perhaps it was buried beneath the gallows, or alternatively smuggled away by friends and interred at either Naseby Field or in the grounds of his daughter's house in Northborough, seven miles from Peterborough. There are also a group of historians who believe the most credible claim is that for Newburgh Priory in Yorkshire, which for years was the home of the Wombwell family, descendants of Cromwell. But, once again, there is no conclusive answer to this mystery, either...

However, all this talk in Woodbridge about the 'devil's skull', coupled with Canon Wilkinson's remark about the evidence for Cromwell's pact with Satan being contained in an old volume of history, made me keen to examine the book. I finally located a copy in the British Museum, after a curious experience while looking at the subject-index of the catalogue in the reading room. For there under the word 'Devil', the very first entry that caught my eye read: 'See Oliver Cromwell, The Protector.'

While I was still pondering over this unexpected association, I came across the entry for the book I was seeking and shortly I had in my hands a massive 270-year-old folio volume, bearing on its first page the imposing title, *The History of England. From the Beginning of the Reign of King Charles the First to the Restoration of King Charles the Second*. Beneath this the author was given as one Laurence Echard, A.M. Arch-deacon of Stowe.

Interestingly, Echard proved to be a man local to our story, having been born at Barham near Beccles, in Norfolk, in about the year 1670. He had apparently become an archdeacon at Stowe in 1712, and it was his passion for recent history that had resulted in the writing of this massive tome, which he had published in 1718. It was based, Echard said in his introduction, on contemporary documents and the memories of people still living – and is therefore obviously all the more valuable as a source of reference. On page 712, I came across the lines to which Canon Wilkinson had undoubtedly been referring. (I have reproduced Echard's quaint prose exactly as printed, save replacing the inevitable 'f' of this period with 's'.)

We have a strange Story which the Author says he received from a Person of Quality, viz. 'It was believed and that not without some good Cause, that Cromwell the same Morning that he defeated the King's Army at Worcester, had Conference personally with the Devil, with whom he made a Contract, that to have his Will then, and in all Things else for Seven Years from that Day, he should, at the Expiration of the said Year, have him at his Command, to do as his Pleasure, both with his Soul and Body.'

This is also related in other printed Books; but we have received a more full Account never yet published, which is here inserted as a Thing more wonderful than probable, and therefore more for the Diversion than Satisfaction of the reader. It is a relation or Narrative of a valient Officer called Lindsey, an intimate Friend of Cromwell's, the first Captain of his Regiment, and therefore commonly called Colonel Lindsey, which is to this effect.

'On the 3rd of September in the morning, Cromwell took this Officer to a Wood Side not far from the Army, and bid him alight and follow him into the Wood, and to take particular Notice of what he saw and heard. After they had both alighted, and secured their horses, and walked some small way into the Wood, Lindsey began to turn pale, and to be seized with horror from some unknown Cause: Upon which Cromwell asked him, How he did, or how he felt himself. He answered, That he was in such a Trembling and Consternation that he never felt the like in all the Conflicts and Battles he had been engaged in; but whether it proceeded from the Gloominess of the Place, or the Temperament of his Body, he knew not. How now, said Cromwell, what, troubled with Vapours? Come forwards, Man!

'They had not gone above Twenty Yards, before Lindsey on a sudden stood still, and cried out, By all that's good, he was seized with such unaccountable Terror and Astonishment, that it was impossible for him to stir one Step further. Upon which Cromwell called him, Faint-hearted Fool, and bid him stand there and observe, or be Witness; and then advancing some Distance from him, he met with a grave, elderly Man with a Roll of Parchment in his Hand, who delivered it to Cromwell, who eagerly perused it.

'Lindsey, a little recovered from his Fear, heard several loud Words between them: particularly Cromwell said, This is but for Seven Years; I was to have had it for One and Twenty, and it must and shall be so. The other told him positively, it could not be for above Seven; upon which Cromwell cried with great Fierceness, It should however be for Fourteen Years. But the other peremptorily declared, it could not possibly be for any longer Time; and if he would not take it so, there were Others who would accept of it. Upon which Cromwell at last took the Parchment, and returning to Lindsey with great Joy in his Countenance, he cried, Now, Lindsey, the Battle is our own! I long to be engaged.

'Returning out of the Wood, they rode to the Army, Cromwell with a Resolution to engage as soon as possible, and the other with a Design of leaving the Army as soon. After the first Charge, Lindsey deserted his Post, and rode away with all possible speed, Day and Night, till he came into the County of Norfolk, to the House of an intimate Friend, one Mr Thorowgood, Minister of the Parish of [Here there is a curious blank space in the printed text, of which more anon] Cromwell as soon as he missed Lindsey, sent all Ways after him, with a Promise of a great Reward to any that should bring him alive or dead.'

Thus far is the Narrative of Lindsey himself; but something further is to be remembered, to complete and confirm the Story. When Mr Thorowgood saw his Friend Lindsey come into his Yard, his Horse and Himself just tired, in a sort of amaze, said, How now, Colonel! We hear there is like to be a Battle shortly; what, fled from your Colours? A Battle! said the other, yes there has been a Battle, and I am sure the King is beaten; but if ever I strike a Stroke for Cromwell again may I perish eternally: For I am sure he has made a League with the Devil, and the Devil will have him in due Time.

Then desiring his Protection from Cromwell's Inqui-
sitors, he went in and related to him the whole Story, and
all the Circumstances, concluding with these remarkable
words, That Cromwell would certainly die that Day seven
Years that the Battle was fought. The Strangeness of the
Relation caused Mr Thorowgood to order his son John,
then about Twelve Years of Age, to write it in full length in
his Common-Place Book, and to take it from Lindsey's
own Mouth. This Common-Place Book, and likewise the
same Story written in other Books, I am assured is still
preserved in the family of the Thorowgoods. But how far
Lindsey is to be believed, and how far the Story is to be
accounted incredible, is left to the Reader's Faith and
Judgement and not to any determination of our own.

This story seemed just as remarkable to me, a late
twentieth century reader, as it must have done to those
who had perused Echard's words two centuries earlier.
What puzzled me, though, was why the Reverend
Thorowgood's parish had not been identified – or,
alternatively, if it had been deliberately left out.
Subsequent enquiry has convinced me that the man was
Thomas Thorowgood, the rector of Little Massingham,
near King's Lynn, who was a staunch supporter of the
Cromwellians and a member of their 'Assembly of Divines'.
What I could not unearth from these facts was anything
further about how Thorowgood had reacted to Lindsey's
story – so instead I turned to a modern historian, Ronald
Holmes, author of one of the most relevant works on the
period, *Witchcraft in British History* (1974) to see if he could
throw any further light on the legend.

'There's no doubt that the whole story of Cromwell's
rise from the position of a country squire to the equivalent
of the king of England was so startling that there seemed
no explanation other than that he had dealings with the
devil,' he told me. 'Remember, too, that he quite openly
believed that September 3rd was his lucky day. On that
date he began the siege of Drogheda in 1649, fought the
Battle of Dunbar in 1650, and then Worcester in 1651 – all
of which were successes. And it was, of course, the date

on which it is said he made his pact with the Devil.'

Ronald then pointed out that the date of Cromwell's death in 1658 was also 3 September and the significance of this was quite clearly not lost on those people of the time who studied such things. Within a few years, he says, superstitious tales had begun to circulate that the devil had come for his own. Holmes added a further interesting point.

'By some dramatic coincidence the spring and summer of Cromwell's last year was icy cold,' he said, 'and it was probably because of this that the supposed omen appeared which was said to have foretold his death. In June a great whale found its way south and entered the Thames where sailors attacked it and it died after giving out a horrible groan. It was also believed that dogs barked all through the night Cromwell died and that his death was heralded by a most terrible storm – traditionally the sign of the passing of a magician.'

It seems clear to me today that while the mystery of the whereabouts of Oliver Cromwell's skull may have at last been laid to rest – though one cannot be quite so sure that its influence is not still active in Woodbridge – the larger issue as to whether the protector was in league with the devil remains unsolved. I suggest, however, that if there is one other piece of evidence that might finally settle the issue then it may just be found, appropriately, in East Anglia at the Norris Library in St Ives to which I was directed during my research.

In the library's collection of documents is a handwritten manuscript by a former resident of St Ives, Edmund Pettis, who lived there at the end of the seventeenth and the beginning of the eighteenth century, when much of the work was committed to paper. The contents are mostly about the history of St Ives, but because Oliver Cromwell lived in the town for a while Pettis copied into his book some letters written between Cromwell and his most intimate friend, the army chaplain Hugh Peters, during the last days of the king's life. (Charles, of course, died on the scaffold on 30 January 1649).

In prefacing the letters, Pettis assures any reader of their authenticity, for they were, he says, 'copy'd from that wrote with Oliver Cromwell's own hand'. Let me quote from the two most relevant – and crucial – pieces of correspondence. The first is from Cromwell to Peters and is dated 'Westminster, January 25, 1649':

Friend of my Bosom,
    I greatly rejoice to see this blessed day wherein we have completed the work of the Lord in condemning the wicked Charles Stuart to die for his manifold transgressions. I believe its evidently known to you and all that espouse our righteous cause how great an instrument I was in subduing the tyrant. But then it was by such means which will seem no less strange to you, then somewhat uneasy to me.
    But as I can trust you with the secret which I conjure you never to reveal to any, I must confess to you that when I first entered upon a military employment to relieve my injured country from oppression, the day after I received my commission walking in the evening in Hyde Park the Devil appeared to me in human shape and upon promises of assuring me always success over my enemies, the honour thereof tempted me to sell my soul and body to him. But not to take possession thereof thirty-nine years commencing from the day and date of our contract.
    But though he has punctually hitherto observed his articles on his part (yet it is my opinion and I also desire yours in ye next letter) that I am not in conscience bound to stand to my obligation because the cause which I fought for was not his, for he encourages popery, tyranny, arbitrary power and wicked Princes. Therefore the contract is null and void. But let it be as it will I desire your advice in it and in ye meantime I rest the true and constant hearer of your soul saving doctrine.'

The letter is signed 'Oliver Cromwell'. The Protector did not have to wait long for his reply, which came from his chaplain datelined with the words 'London, January 29, 1649.'

Precious Man,
    Yours I received wherein you have disclosed a secret (which I promise you) shall die with me. What you have

done in defence of our cause is allowable and praiseworthy for had you as many Souls and Bodies as you have Men under your command the Bargain for what you sold them for was worth the price. Considering it was to deliver yourself and us from Popery, Slavery and Arbitrary power. However assure yourself that Satan has no power over you because he was the occasion of all that Bloodshed by your enemies and encouraged them to ruin and destroy our country.

I suppose you have something from under the roaring lion's hand for performance of his promise which I exhort you to burn now the glorious work is done. The fervent prayers of our congregation shall make your contract with him of no effect. This is all at present telling you I think every minute a year till tomorrow when Charles Stuart is sent out of this world.

The letter ends with a flourish from 'your sincear spirituall (sic) Friend – Hugh Peters.'

Edmund Pettis adds a caustic footnote of his own. 'By these letters,' he writes, 'and all their canting it plainly appears that this fanatical crew used all possible means in the whole course of their proceedings by base and vile insinuations to cheat the people so now you see how they are also trying to trick the Devil!'

While, of course, this correspondence suggests that Cromwell had actually made this pact with the devil in London well before the battle of Worcester, it is certainly a far more sensational – and damning – piece of evidence, for the other story is based solely on the testimony of one man, Colonel Lindsey. It might also be argued of Cromwell's later actions that once he had received his note of 'absolution' from Hugh Peters he used it as an excuse to remove all thought of devil worship from his mind ... and his life.

Be that as it may, just as the Lord Protector's head was condemned to wander the centuries trying to find rest, so the legend of its owner's involvement with the powers of darkness was similarly destined to continue arousing interest: all the more so since it was publicly revealed in Woodbridge. And whether the case is proved or will remain another of the mysteries of history – not to mention the 'supernatural coast' – I leave the reader to judge for himself...

# 8   The Witch Finder of Mistley

Mistley seems a most aptly named place on a dark winter's day when shards of grey fog are easing their way in from the North Sea across the cluster of houses and maritime buildings which make up this small port. All the more so when the visitor learns of the sinister associations the community has with stories of witch-hunting and the persistent ghost of a man who terrorized East Anglia over three hundred years ago.

Situated on the Stour estuary not far from Harwich, Mistley is today a busy little port trading in timber, grain and soya flour. In popular legend, however, it is known as the place where the infamous Matthew Hopkins, 'The Witch Finder General', had his headquarters for his brutal campaign of persecution in the seventeenth century, and where, so the stories go, he has remained to haunt ever since. Though there are few physical signs of his evil existence, his brooding figure does rather seem to cling to the place – in particular on bleak winter days – providing yet another example of the enduring power of the supernatural on the imagination.

Driving into Mistley via the A137 from Colchester, a visitor's eyes are immediately drawn to the handsome architecture of its buildings, while his nostrils are assailed by a smell which, it transpires, comes from a factory making malt extract. Almost as quickly his attention will be caught by the sight of the Thorn Hotel, a large, stolid-looking, grey building which faces out across Mistley Quay. But on entering this former coaching inn, with its beams and welcoming bar, obviously much altered during its four hundred years of existence, any visitor would probably be surprised to learn that they had stepped into the very heart of the Hopkins legend. For it was here that the 'Witch Finder' was first based and, in one of its upstairs rooms, conducted some of his earliest and most merciless inquisitions of suspects.

But this said, the Thorn Hotel is none the less an ideal place at which to begin unravelling the story of Matthew Hopkins and his continuing association with Mistley and the adjoining town of Manningtree...

Mistley's link with the supernatural seems to have been almost predestined, for its name is believed to mean 'Mistletoe Wood'. Mistletoe, of course, has a strong association with those ancient mystics, the Druids. The first houses here were probably built at what is now Mistley Heath, and although the tidal channel of the River Stour had long before cut into the sandy cliffs to form a natural harbour at Thorn Reach, it was not until the eighteenth century that the quays and old maltings which make up the present port were built. For this reason, local people insist the proper name of their community is actually Mistley Thorn.

In the years prior to this date, Manningtree – just two miles further up river – was the major trading port of the area, and it was the arrival in the 1770's of one Richard Rigby, a wealthy Member of Parliament and Paymaster General of the army under George III, which transformed Mistley. He decided to use his money to turn the community into the only planned Georgian port in England, complete with its own salt-water spa – and to aid him in this vision he employed one of the great architects of the age, Robert Adam. Though Rigby unfortunately ran out of money before his grandiose scheme could be completed and then died in 1788 leaving no heir, there is evidence of what was achieved at every turn.

First, there is the quay itself where the visitor can see some of the dressed Portland stone that Adam imported especially for the project, and from which ships now come and go on the tide to destinations such as London, Holland and even the Baltic coast. Then, just to the rear of a row of freight sheds which were once part of a sizeable shipyard, there are two curious, identical towers standing incongruously in the middle of a graveyard. These porticoed stone constructions are not the remnants of some giant ornate tomb, but additions made by Adam to what was then the town's rather plain brick parish church. Inexplicably, though, the church was allowed to fall into disrepair, the nave being demolished in 1870, but the towers at least were retained as intriguing reminders of Rigby's scheme. Not far from here is the equally curiously named 'Hopping Bridge' for which the ingenious architect designed the brickwork. This name, incidentally, has nothing to do with either the activity of children or the raw material for beer. The word 'hop' in this instance refers to a marshy enclosure.

In the middle of Mistley itself is a village green around which Adam built a row of small houses for local tradesmen. Then in the centre of the High Street stands the eye-catching pavilion known as Swan House. In front of it is a large ornamental pond complete with a strikingly lifelike swan: all that remains of Rigby's plan for a salt-water bathing pool. Swans are, in fact, a particular feature of Mistley, for a colony of over 400 mute swans live under official protection on the river-bank and can be seen resting or wading all along the shore – especially near the tree-lined road, The Walls, which runs to Manningtree and offers those who stroll along it spectacular views of the estuary.

Immediately opposite the Swan fountain is the Thorn Hotel which originally had bay-fronted windows (now covered by a typical Victorian façade) and which was for many years a popular coaching inn on what was then the main London to Harwich road. According to local sources, it is the only inn of that name in the whole country, and takes its title 'from the furze growth that surrounded it in the days when Matthew Hopkins was the owner.' (Today's inn sign, though, shows a man's hand extracting a thorn from a lion's paw.)

A century ago, Mistley possessed at least two dozen inns like the Thorn to cater for the thirsty seamen who crowded the port. Although Robert Adam left his handiwork on most of the seven which stood in the immediate vicinity of the Swan fountain, only the one allegedly 'owned by Matthew Hopkins' has survived as licensed premises to the present day.

It might perhaps be argued that history should remember Mistley for the unique examples of the work of Robert Adam it contains – or even for the fine ships built here to fight the Spanish Armada and the Napoleonic Wars, including Nelson's magnificent flagship, the 914 ton 'Amphion'. Yet it is the infamy of Matthew Hopkins who put his stamp on the locality almost one hundred years ago which nowadays excites public interest.

When beginning to look at the facts of Hopkins' notoriety, one of the most curious elements which emerges is that records of the cases of many of those he persecuted for witchcraft still exist, but there is not very much to go on about the man himself. Indeed, according to those accounts there are, he was a rather mysterious figure. One of the first Mistley residents I talked to about him told me there were people in the area who had always thought of him as a kind of 'Human Phantom', so incredible were many of the stories told about him and his evil deeds. Such claims are, indeed, to some extent augmented by the famous work of reference, *The Dictionary of National Biography*, which states quite unequivocally, 'Little is known of Hopkins prior to 1644.'

However, in recent years research by several East Anglian historians has resulted in the unearthing of a number of interesting facts about the man. Perhaps most fascinating of all, an engraving of Hopkins has come to light showing the 'Witch Finder' conducting one of his inquisitions of suspected witches in the upstairs front room of a building that is, in all probability, the Thorn Inn.

This depiction of Hopkins is all the more important when considered in relation to the sightings of a ghost in the vicinity to which we shall return later. In the picture he is shown in a broad-brimmed, pointed hat, a flowing Geneva cloak and the boots of a Puritan trooper. Hopkins undoubtedly wore this outfit to give himself an air of authority, and as he swept through the countryside in search of witches, his face almost hooded by the hat and the cloak billowing around him, he must indeed have seemed, to simple-minded countryfolk, an almost super-human figure.

According to local research, in particular that of Mr W.S.Fitch of Ipswich published in the scholarly journal *Notes & Queries*, this extraordinary man was born in 1620, the son of the Reverend James Hopkins, minister of Great Wenham, a small village close to the Suffolk-Essex border. Matthew was the fourth of six children of the minister and his wife, Marie, a woman apparently of French Huguenot stock. Keeping such a large family on the meagre pay of a minister of a tiny parish must have strained the Reverend Hopkins' resources and it seems evident that although Matthew received a basic education – including learning to write English and read Latin – he did not go to university. Several historians of witchcraft have claimed that the young man trained to be a lawyer, but there is no evidence of anyone of his name qualifying in the profession at this time. What seems more likely is that he gained a working knowledge of the law when he left home to become apprenticed as a clerk to a ship-owner in Mistley.

Hopkins was probably in his late teens when he first set eyes on the little riverside community that was to play such an important part in his life – just as he was on it. Richard Deacon, who has made a special study of Hopkins' life, has written in *Witch Finder General* (1976):

> It was a strange, distraught and curiously notorious neighbourhood into which Hopkins moved and it was also the centre of a widespread area with a reputation for witchcraft and crime. There are more stories even today of hauntings in this part of Essex than almost any other. The crime was almost certainly linked with the shipping trade and smugglers. Apart from this, Manningtree and Mistley were besmirched by some of the most violent and brutal religious dissensions and 'crimes' of the sixteenth and seventeenth century. 'Manningtree rogues' and 'Mistley malcontents' were phrases often used during this period.

It is not too difficult to imagine the young Hopkins rubbing shoulders with the ill-assorted men and women who populated this little community at that time, many showing the signs of mental instability brought on by generations of inbreeding. The mortality rate among infants was high, the appalling sanitary conditions went hand in glove with disease, and the young looked old long before their time. It comes as no surprise, therefore, to learn that the facial twitches, bodily contortions and physical markings brought about by years of incestuous relationships were to become, in his eyes, the proof of witchcraft.

Matthew's work as an articled clerk set him above many of the folk in Mistley, and though we have no knowledge of how he spent his time when not working, he was certainly a devoted reader. There is clear evidence of this by the number of books he referred to when he took up the study of witchcraft. In the year 1641, when he became twenty-one, there is also evidence that he came into some money from the will of his father who had died a few years earlier in Great Wenham. Mr W.S.Fitch claims that Hopkins used this money to buy some property in Mistley, 'including an interest in the old Thorn Inn' where he thereafter lived.

There is further proof of this statement in a manuscript which is entitled in the typical, long-winded style of the time, *Revelation and Narrations of Observations of Matters of Fact and Opinion Concerning Witchcraft and Political Controversies in the Tendring Hundred District*, compiled by various writers between 1645 and 1650. In this it is stated that Hopkins, 'set himselfe up at Mistley Thorn Inn which place he embraced for his conspiracies and to which came his manie informers against the Witches.'

The Civil War beween Charles I and his royalist supporters and Oliver Cromwell and his parliamentarians, was almost two years old when Matthew Hopkins began his campaign against the witches of East Anglia. Already the area had been thrown into turmoil as a result of the fighting, because although the Puritan cause was the better supported, both ideas had followers in Mistley.

Quite what made Hopkins decide to pursue a career catching witches is debatable. There is, however, credible evidence to suggest that from childhood he had heard stories about witchcraft, as it was a popular topic of conversation in Essex and Suffolk. We also know that he read King James I study, *Daemonolgie, The Lancashire Witches' Trial* of 1612 by James I. Potts, and the Reverend Richard Bernard's *Guide Book to Grand Jury Men* which was to become his *vide mecum* when he began his prosections. So did he imagine himself the instrument of a great crusade to rid the country of witches in the same manner as Cromwell was eliminating the royalists? Or was he simply an opportunist who saw a chance to make himself wealthy and famous?

East Anglian historian Frederick Ross in *Bygone Essex* (1892) is in no doubt.

Matthew Hopkins was a vile imposter, unscrupulous, unprincipled, and utterly regardless of the sufferings he inflicted on others, so long as he could put money in his own pocket. He was better remembered than the other witch finders perhaps by being more audacious and insolent, and less observant of the restraints of religion, morality or decorum, than such as had adopted the profession without altogether throwing off the scruples of conscience and the ordinary rules of civil communities.

A recent writer, the American historian, Edward D.Hoch, has, however, addressed the question of Hopkins in a perhaps more objective way. In his article, *Matthew Hopkins: Witch-Finder General*, published in 1979, he writes:

It is perhaps one of the oddities of British history that the year 1645 saw both an event as sublime as the publication of John Milton's collected Poems and one as sinister as the reign of Matthew Hopkins, the so-called Witch-Finder General. If Milton's poems have had the more lasting effect on Western civilisation, the brief and terrible career of Hopkins was not without its wide-ranging shock waves. Some historians have even argued that the witch-hunting hysteria nurtured by Hopkins was one of the direct causes of the Salem witchcraft trials in New England half a century later.

The national mood was right for a man like Hopkins in that year. England was torn by Civil War and King Charles was but a few short years from the executioner's axe. Essex was the centre of tensions at the time, and the headquarters for Cromwell's puritanical Roundheads. It was therefore easy for a man like Hopkins, eager to improve his fortunes and in need of money, to announce to the authorities that he possessed the Devil's own list of all the witches in England and offer his services as a witch finder.

The evidence of Hopkins' later career certainly supports the view that he earned his notoriety through a mixture of cunning, intelligence and persuasion, not to mention a streak of sadism, a predilection for torture and an unholy love of money. Where Edward D.Hoch is not quite correct is in giving 1645 as the date of the start of Hopkins' reign of terror. In fact, he had begun his work at least a year earlier according to the tract he himself published in 1647, entitled *The Discoverie of Witches*.

The Discoverer [i.e. Hopkins himself] never travelled far for it, but in March 1644 he had some seven or eight of that horrible sect of Witches living in the town where he lived, a town in Essex called Manningtree, with divers other adjacent Witches of other towns, who every six weeks in the night (being always on the Friday night) had their meeting close by his house, and had their several solemn sacrifices there offered to the Devil, one of which this discoverer heard speaking to her Imps one night, and bid them go to another Witch, who was thereupon apprehended, and searched by women who had for many years known the Devil's marks, and found to have three teats about her, which honest women have not: so upon command from the Justice, they were to keep her from sleep two or three nights, expecting in that time to see her familiars, which the fourth night he called in by their several names, and told them what shapes, a quarter of an hour before they came in, there being ten of us in the room.

Hopkins goes on to describe these various 'imps' which appeared in the room – creatures which were in all probability nothing more dangerous than a kitten, a spaniel, a greyhound, a black rabbit and a polecat. All the kind of animals one might well expect to find in Mistley, especially in the vicinity of the Thorn Inn if, as I believe, that was where Hopkins carried out this inquiry.

Although it seems evident from his statement that Hopkins was hoping to be able to uncover whole covens of witches, it is curious that at no time did he attempt to capture any such groups redhanded. In fact, his first victim was a solitary old woman known as 'Mother Clarke', one of the most pathetic figures to be found in Mistley who was at least eighty years old, had not a tooth in her head and had suffered the added misfortune of losing a leg. To damn Mother Clarke further, her own mother had been hanged for alleged witchcraft, and she begged coins around the village by telling highly fanciful stories of her parent's activities.

Hopkins treatment of this unfortunate crone was to be typical of many of his later operations.

The case against Elizabeth Clarke was that she had bewitched one of her neighbour's wives and caused the women to suffer a mysterious illness. Hopkins took it upon himself to bring Clarke to his rooms and there had her searched for witches' marks. Having satisfied himself that a wart close to her breast was a 'devil's teat' he swore out information against the old woman and obtained the authority of the magistrates to extract a confession from her. Using a mixture of torture and blandishments he made the muddled and frightened old woman admit that not only was she in league with the devil, but had also regularly had sexual intercourse with him. To Hopkins' obvious delight, Mother Clarke also implicated one of her neighbours, Anne West, claiming that she, too, had had sex with the devil.

Historian Richard Deacon, writing of Hopkins concentration on sexual evidence in his cases against suspected witches says, 'He possessed a strong anti-feminist bias and an obsession with sex – a dangerous combination –

and he was also anxious to imitate the continental practice in witchcraft trials of alleging sexual intercourse with the Devil. Hopkins was shrewd enough to realise that the Puritan justices of the area would find such allegations abhorrent.'

Fired with enthusiasm at having apprehended Elizabeth Clarke and Anne West, Hopkins next began to scour the neighbourhood for other witches, hauling his victims back to Mistley for interrogation in the Thorn Inn. And aided by gossip, hearsay and unashamed prejudice, he had, by July 1645, uncovered a total of thirty-two witches who were sent for trial to Chelmsford. To help convict these women he also assembled no fewer than ninety-two witnesses.

A local legend in Mistley maintains that two days before the trial opened on 29 July, a group of these accused witches, including the aforementioned Elizabeth Clarke and Anne West, plus Anne Leech and Elizabeth Gooding who were also local women, conspired to 'send a bear to kill Hopkins in his garden.' Presumably this refers to the garden at the rear of the Thorn Inn, but there are no facts to corroborate the story – and certainly Hopkins was in no way intimidated by the threat if there *was* any truth in it!

At the trial in Chelmsford, the women were variously accused of 'bewitching to death' and 'entertaining evil spirits', and the court records indicate that nineteen were sentenced to death, eight were remanded in custody until the next sessions, four died in prison during the course of the trial, and only one was acquitted. This sole survivor was Rebecca West, the daughter of Anne West, who had apparently led the Witch Finder to many of his victims: in return, it would seem, for her own freedom. For she, too, had admitted to Hopkins while condemning her own mother that she had 'sold her soul' to the devil and actually entered into a marriage with him.

According to most versions of Hopkins' life, immediately after the successful outcome of this trial he was appointed official 'Witch Finder General' by a grateful parliament in Westminster and given cart blanche to root out and bring to justice witches wherever he found them. In fact, there is no evidence whatsoever that he was given

such a title officially, and although the authorities may
well have quietly acquiesced to his campaign, the title
'Witch Finder General' was undoubtedly bestowed upon
Hopkins by ... himself.

At this juncture, Hopkins also decided to employ two
assistants, John Stearne and Mary Phillips, to help him in
his 'campaign'. Both were from nearby Manningtree:
Stearne a single-minded Puritan who believed implicitly
in the existence of the devil, and Mary Phillips, a
practicing midwife whose task it was to spot the devil's
marks on the women accused of witchcraft. From that
summer of 1645, this unholy trio were hardly ever seen
apart, especially when interrogating their victims.

By Hopkins' own admission, one of his favourite
methods for establishing proof of witchcraft was by
'swimming' a suspect in a pond – a method he is said to
have adopted from Continental cases which he had read
about and was the first to introduce into England. But
since floating was viewed as proof of witchcraft and
sinking resulted in death, if the woman was not pulled
quickly enough to the surface, the unfortunate victim had
little chance of survival either way! Conveniently, a pond
ideally suited for the Witch Finder's needs was to be found
a short walk from the Thorn Inn on Mistley Heath, a spot
not far from where the new church of St Mary's & St
Michael's stands today. This locality will feature in our
story again.

An account of one such swimming has been provided in
an old manuscript written by a Dr Harold Deacon which is
now lodged in the Essex Records Office. In this, the author
refers specifically to the case of a Mrs Lacy who, after a
'devil's mark' had been found on her body, was bound
hand and foot and taken in a cart to the pond. Dr Deacon
goes on:

> It is well known that the vileness of witches is such that
> water, the purest of all elements, invariably refuses to have
> anything to do with them. Obviously, then, you have only
> to throw a witch into a pond to have any doubt which you
> may entertain as to her guilt cleared up immediately by
> ocular demonstration.

Mrs Lacy admirably responded to this test. She floated for quite a considerable time; and though sceptics nowadays will doubtless suggest that this, in view of her voluminous skirts, was merely what might have been expected, Mr Hopkins knew better. The effect of this experiment, taken in conjunction with the discovery by Mr Hopkins of the Devil's Mark, would in itself have been sufficient to send anyone to the gallows.

As Hopkins and his cohorts began to travel further afield so the variety of their methods of torture grew – likewise the Witch Finder General's purse. In order to achieve confessions, Hopkins would either starve his suspects, deprive them of sleep, tie them cross-legged on stools in an agony of cramp, or even march them backwards and forwards on blistered feet for hours on end until they broke down and agreed to whatever he suggested.

Hearing about Hopkins' 'work', a number of rural communities in East Anglia began to call on his services, and it is evident that he varied his fees considerably from £5 for the smallest village to £23 for the larger towns. (This at a time when the average wage was sixpence per day!) His expenses when staying in these communities were also to be paid by the parish officials. Witchcraft expert Ronald Seth in his book, *Stories of Great Witch Trials* (1967) has estimated that during the three years that Hopkins was operational he probably earned somewhere in the region of £60,000 to £100,000 by today's standards.

An interesting document that has survived from this period is a letter by Hopkins addressed to a magistrate at Great Staughton in Huntingdonshire where he had been invited to visit. Here it is in full:

My services to your Worship presented, I have this day received a letter to come to a Town called Great Staughton to search for evil disposed persons called Witches (though I hear your Minister is far against us through ignorance). I intend to come (God willing) the sooner to hear his singular judgement on behalf of such parties. I have known a Minister in Suffolk preach as much against their Discovery in a pulpit, and forced to recant it (by the

Committee) in the same place. I much marvelled such evil members should have any (much more any of the clergy) who should daily preach Terror to convince such offenders, stand up to take their parts, against such as are complainants for the King and Sufferers themselves, with their families and Estates.

I intend to give your town a visit suddenly. I come to Kimbolton this week, and it shall be ten to one, but I will come to your town first, but I would certainly know afore whether your town affords many Sticklers for such Cattell, or willing to give and afford us good welcome and entertainment, as otherwise I have been, else I shall wave your Shire (not as yet beginning in any part of it myself) and betake to such places where I do, and may persist without control, but with Thanks and Recompense. So I humbly take my leave, and rest,

Your Servant to be Commanded,
Matthew Hopkins.

What is particularly interesting about this letter is Hopkins' mention of the hostility to his cause of the town's unnamed minister. In fact, the man was a certain Reverend John Gaule who was to play a crucial role in bringing the Witch Finder's career to an end – of which more anon.

After their successes in Essex, Hopkins and his colleagues next turned their attentions to Norfolk and Suffolk, then to Cambridge, Northampton, Huntingdon and Bedford. Another historian, Eric Maple, has written in *The Dark World of Witches* (1962):

The witch finders ravaged almost the whole of East Anglia, operating upon a commercial basis rather in the manner of a rat-catcher with vermin. Often their presence in a district was sufficient to bring forth a flood of denunciation from vindictive villagers against local scapegoats, some of whom, in a desperate attempt to clear their names, actually volunteered to undergo the swimming test, believing it would vindicate them – and were hanged for their credulity. Meggs, a Suffolk baker, offered himself to be searched for witches' marks. These were found and he was executed.

Suffolk, in fact, probably suffered worst at Hopkins' hands, nearly 200 persons being arrested for suspected witchcraft, sixty-eight of whom were tried and hung. Although the total of women that he brought to the gallows will probably never be accurately known, 'several hundreds' is the guess of Rossell Hope Robins in his *Encyclopedia of Witchcraft and Demonology* (1959). What remains undeniable is that in his three year career, the former clerk from Mistley put more suspected witches to death than were hung by all the other witch-hunters in 160 years of persecution.

Inevitably, of course, voices began to be raised in protest at this wholesale slaughter of feeble-minded old women on the most absurd evidence, and the first man to seriously challenge Hopkins' 'cause' was the Huntingdonshire clergyman John Gaule, who began to deliver sermons against the Witch Finder in the spring of 1646.

Later that year, Gaule, himself a strong willed Puritan, went further and published a tract entitled *An Exposure of Some of the Nefarious Acts of Witch-Finders*, in which he denounced Hopkins' methods – in particular the 'swimming test' – and revealed the horrors being done in the name of religion. When a copy of this publication reached the 'Witch Finder General' during a break from his travels in Mistley, he set to work on a rebuttal to Gaule's accusations which he entitled *The Discovery of Witches* and published early the following year.

The book was, though, little more than an attempted justification for his relentless pursuit of witches based on selected quotations from the Bible and his own interpretation of the statutes contained in the Reverend Bernard's *Guide to Jury Men*.

But to the undoubted relief of many people in East Anglia, John Gaule's crusade gradually had the desired effect. A Parliamentary Commission was set up to enquire into Hopkins' methods and while it upheld the principle of witch hunts it outlawed the use of the 'swimming' of suspects. This judgement – plus the fact that his influence was clearly beginning to be undermined due to the sheer

numbers of suspected witches he was bringing to court
and the fact that even the most credulous judges were
starting to question his evidence and his fees – made
Hopkins decide his own days were numbered.

So a few months later, he quietly returned to the banks
of the Stour estuary with the intention of living out the
rest of his life enjoying his now considerable wealth. His
assistants, John Stearne and Mary Phillips, also decided to
slip from public view wih equal alacrity.

But the story of Matthew Hopkins does not end there.
In fact, where Mistley is concerned it only really begins in
that year of 1647. For exactly how Hopkins died, where he
was buried, and if it is his ghost which has haunted the
district for the last 300 years have all helped to generate a
mystery which has earned the village a special place in
supernatural lore.

Looking through the various accounts of Hopkins' reign
of terror which have been compiled over the intervening
years, it soon becomes apparent that there are three quite
different versions of his death.

The most prosaic of these is that not long after his
'retirement', the Witch Finder contacted tuberculosis and
died in his bed at the Thorn Inn. He was then quietly
interred without fuss or anyone to mourn him in Mistley
Church.

A more popular – and understandably more widely
quoted – story says that Hopkins was actually given a
taste of his own medicine and 'swum' as a witch. The first
report of this is to be found in a work entitled *An
Historical Essay Concerning Witchcraft* written by Bishop
Francis Hutchinson in 1718. He wrote:

> What I have often heard is that Hopkins went on searching
> and swimming poor creatures until some gentleman, out
> of indigntion at the Barbarity, took him and tied his own
> Thumbs and Toes, as he used to tie others, and when he
> was put into the Water, he himself swam as they did. That
> clear'd the Country of him; and it was a great deal of Pity
> that they did not think of the Experiment sooner.

I shall return to this statement that Hopkins 'clear'd the

country' shortly, but there is also a slightly different version of this story by Frederick Ross in *English Witchcraft* (1956).

> When passing through Suffolk during one of his visitations, Hopkins was accused of being in league himself with the Devil, and was charged with having stolen from him a memorandum book containing the list of all the witches in England, which he obtained by means of sorcery. Of course he denied his guilt, but was put by the mob to his own swimming test. Some say he was drowned, others that he floated and was condemned on other evidence and executed. There is no record of his trial, but from that time we hear no more of him, the probability being that he met with his death at the hands of the populace.

Much as one would like to believe that justice had been appropriately served in this manner, there is no definite proof to support Ross's contention. Indeed, it has been suggested by other writers that the whole story may have been an elaboration of a contemporary statement made by Samuel Butler in his famous satire, *Hudibras*, in which he refers to Hopkins and says that he 'after prov'd himself a Witch, And made a Rod for his own Breech'.

Of modern writers, Rossell Hope Robbins in his *Encyclopedia* is inclined to support the views of 'most contemporary writers' who maintained that Hopkins was 'hacked to death by people whom his sadism had offended'. Again there is no factual confirmation of such an event which would surely have been recorded somewhere about a man of Hopkins' notoriety, and the *Dictionary of National Biography* which had so little to say of Hopkins early life is equally terse about his end. 'According to Hutchinson,' it says, 'Hopkin's thumbs and toes were tied, and he swam and was hanged.'

But Bishop Hutchinson did not, in fact, say that the Witch Finder was hanged, as the reader will recall. What he said was that the swimming 'clear'd the Country of him' – which opens up a third possible explanation as to Hopkins' fate: that he quite simply fled the country and was never heard of again. He could, in fact, have quite easily slipped away to the continent on one of the boats sailing from Mistley, and was certainly wealthy enough to be able to assuage the principles of even the most staunchly Puritan captain. I have even heard it suggested that he might ultimately have reached America and there resumed his career under a new identity, when the same witchcraft hysteria that had gripped East Anglia manifested itself in New England.

My own research, however, suggests that the answer to Hopkins' fate lies in Mistley, and with it an explanation of the supernatural manifestations that have been reported in the area during the past three centuries. For I am convinced that the Witch Finder did, indeed, die in the little community and was buried in an unmarked grave on what is now Mistley Heath.

The most important element of my evidence is the register of the parish of Mistley-cum-Manningtree for the years 1550 to 1650 which, though faded and fragile, is still in the keeping of the parish. For amongst the entries for burials during the year 1647 are two lines which read as follows:

1647. Aug 12. Matthew son of Mr James Hopkins, minister of Wenham, buried at Mistley.

Although the entry might seem sparse for such a notorious man, it is perfectly understandable that his 'career' as a Witch Finder was hardly one that the vicar entering the records would want to note. And as we know that Matthew was the son of James Hopkins, the minister of Wenham, there can surely be no doubt that it was he who was buried on that August day.

But then the question follows: where was he buried? That long-winded manuscript of *Revelation in the Tendring Hundred District* which I mentioned earlier provides an indirect, but none the less intriguing, answer.

'Nobodie in the locality was present at hys burial,' the document states, 'and if buried he was at Mistley it may have beene outside the precincts of the Churche in the dark of night when no one else was about his business.'

During the course of my research, I have walked around the area where the old St Mary's Church stood on Mistley Heath though not, I have to add, in the 'dark of night'! It is mainly a heavily wooded area, criss-crossed by narrow tracks which can have changed little since Hopkins' time. But of the graveyard or a headstone which might provide the conclusive piece of evidence there is no sign, for after the church was allowed to fall into disrepair the entire area was bulldozed flat.

What, though, has been seen in the intervening years a number of times is a ghostly figure, described as wearing what seemed like a pointed hat and a flowing cloak. If it *is* the shade of Matthew Hopkins, then is he searching for the grave from which he was so unceremoniously evicted?

In recent years, I learned, several Mistley clergymen have investigated the Hopkins legend, in particular the Reverend Anthony Smith who told me he was convinced that the Witch Finder lay in an unmarked grave somewhere near the old church. He had also heard reports of a ghost in the vicinity of the new St Mary's Church close to the town, but no-one had been able to provide any details as to what it was wearing.

Nor is this the only part of Mistley where the ghost of Matthew Hopkins has been reported. Not far from the new St Mary's on the Manningtree Road is Mistley Pond, a stretch of brown, murky water partly surrounded by reeds and overshadowed by willow trees. It was here that Hopkins 'swam' his victims – and in it, too, that he suffered the same torture, according to local tradition. There are a number of accounts of his ghost being spotted in the vicinity, the most graphic encounter being that of Mr Herbert Bird who lives in nearby Lawford.

I used to work at night driving lorries for a local firm. I would walk along the The Walls to work – I'd done it hundreds of times. Then one night I saw this apparition. It was a man dressed in a flowing cloak and a Cromwellian hat. The figure was about six foot high and it ran across the road and clutched a lamp post. As I walked up level on the opposite side of the road it just vanished. The following day I went back in daylight and studied the grass by the lamp post. There was a patch of thicker, darker grass about six foot by three, like there might be a grave underneath. Anyhow, I reported what I had seen to the police but they said there was nothing they could do. They certainly couldn't go around digging up The Walls for the grave of a ghost! But I know what I saw – and seeing is believing.'

Could this possibly be the site of Hopkins' grave? The idea certainly intrigued the historian Richard Deacon when he heard Herbert Bird's story.

'I visited the site quite recently,' he said. 'The Walls are close to the pond where Matthew was reputed to have been swum, and I have to admit I could imagine that this might well be the grave 'outside the precincts of the church' to which the *Tending Witchcraft Revelations* refers. It seemed not inappropriate to me that the man who made his fortune hunting witches should in the end become a friendless, lonely victim of tuberculosis until death turned him into a restless, tormented soul.'

The people of Mistley, similarly, do not lightly dismiss such stories – a fact which any visitor will find emphasized the moment he or she reaches the Thorn Inn. For in the front window of the Post Office right next door is a picture board of old photographs of the village with a note about the association of Matthew Hopkins and the inn which says, 'IT'S SINISTER PAST IS REFLECTED IN FREQUENT SIGHTINGS OF GHOSTS AND INEXPLICABLE, PERHAPS SUPERNATURAL, HAPPENINGS.'

One person whose experience contributed to this record is Mr Geoff Smithson who lived at the Thorn for a number of years and saw a figure in a pointed hat and cloak sitting in an armchair in an uptairs room. The self-same room in which tradition says Hopkins conducted his inquisition of suspects. Another local man, Mr Rupert Langley, who lives opposite the inn, says he once heard the sound of a person passing through the bead curtains of the bar around midnight some years ago. 'But there was nobody there.'

Yet another local resident, John Fairhill, who has produced an interesting brochure on the history of Mistley, told me that he had heard stories that two former landlords of the Thorn had actually taken photographs of a hooded figure seen in the bar, but unfortunately both had now left the district. Neither man could identify the phantom as definitely being that of Matthew Hopkins, John added.

Poppy Bennett, a clairvoyant who is also the leader of a Spiritualist Church in Mistley, can also add stories about the Thorn Inn ghost which, she says, 'has been heard rattling about at night, usually in one of the upstairs rooms.'

However, her own remarkable experience of Matthew Hopkins occurred not in Mistley, but while she was conducting a séance in 1970 at the Red Lion pub in Manningtree, which is also believed to have associations with the Witch Finder.

'While the séance was in progress I suddenly saw this figure,' she recalls. 'He was wearing dark clothing. He had no hat and was holding a cane. I could see he had lank, oily hair; dark, glittering eyes; and a small beard and moustache. He stared at me for a while and then disappeared. He seemed to be a man of the sixteenth or seventeenth century and I did not realize until afterwards that it had been Matthew Hopkins.'

There are still more folk in Mistley who talk of similar sightings of this mysterious figure near the harbour, beside the road at Mistley Towers and on the hill up to Mistley Heath – all locations where the Witch Finder once walked. Small wonder, then, that following yet another report of a sighting in the port in August 1974 – a few days after the anniversary of Hopkins' death – the local newspaper, *The Harwich and Manningtree Standard* should comment 'This is the haunt – if you'll forgive the word – of old Matthew Hopkins, about whom ghost stories come almost as thick as the falling leaves of autumn – and no two are alike.'

But in spite of their disparity, what all these stories *do* prove is that even if the evil which Hopkins committed is now no more than a memory, his restless shade is continuing to create interest in Mistley and the remarkable chapter of supernatural history that has been written there...

# 9    The Phantom Centurion
## of Mersea Island

Mersea Island lies on the Essex coast like a small world all of its own. It is linked to the mainland by a tenuous roadway, the Strood, over which high tides quite often sweep, isolating the community just as effectively now as they have done for many centuries. It was, indeed, with good reason that the Romans named the place, Meresaia, 'The Isle of the Sea'.

When the Strood (pronounced hereabouts as 'The Strode') is seen by night with a full moon bathing in the dark, limpid waters as they ebb and flow across the causeway, it is not difficult to believe that it is the location of one of the best known and strangest ghost stories in all East Anglia. The phantom is said to be that of a Roman centurion and a strong element of authenticity is added to the legend by the fact that the island was once occupied by Roman legions. In addition, the nearest big community on the mainland is Colchester: the oldest recorded town in Britain and the site of the first major Roman settlement in the country.

The ghost of Mersea Island is certainly no ordinary spirit in either his appearance or the activities he is said to perform. Some eye-witnesses say they have seen the figure in full Roman military regalia, while others claim to have heard only the sound of marching feet passing by, accompanied by the unmistakable clanking of military armour. A third group maintain they have sensed other ghostly legionnaires in the company of the centurion – the little contingent apparently fighting a rear-guard action against invaders of the island.

What is, though, universally accepted about this Roman warrior is that he patrols the length of the Strood and has been experienced both on the island and on the mainland, where it joins the major road to Colchester. This road follows the line of the first highway the Romans built outside their fortress at Colchester almost two thousand years ago: an arrow-straight, six mile long roadway that linked the town to Mersea and the North Sea beyond.

There is plenty of evidence to be found in modern day Colchester of the Roman occupation of this part of East Anglia. Ancient fortress walls can still be seen around the outskirts of the town, and in the Castle Museum are all manner of artifacts from the first century AD allowing visitors to step back into early British history.

The evidence indicates that the high ground on which the town stands was originally the site of the British capital of Camulodunum from which the pre-Roman kings ruled the south-east of England. Then in AD 43 the Romans arrived and established a fortress of their own, extending their influence into the countryside and as far as Mersea Island on the coast. According to legend the island was for some years the residence of a Roman general who styled himself 'The Count of the Saxon Shore'.

Colchester's later history – including the attack in AD 61 by the formidable Queen Boadicea during her unsuccessful attempt to rid the nation of the Roman invader, and the famous seige during the Civil War – need not concern us here. The town today, with its busy streets and packed shopping precincts seems far removed from the spirit of Roman times when compared to timeless Mersea – a fact that the relentlessly marching centurion's ghost would seem to emphasize.

Crossing to Mersea by way of the Strood, over the creek known as the Pyefleet Channel, it is easy for a visitor to appreciate why it must have appealed to the Romans and the other invaders who followed in their wake. Oval in shape and five miles long by almost two miles wide, it presents a picture of open pasture-land and well-wooded slopes which disguise most of the modern building on the seaward side. The island is, in fact, divided into two medieval parishes, East and West Mersea: the eastern sector predominantly marshland and the west a more built-up area popular with holidaymakers, fishermen and sailors.

The first soldiers from Rome no doubt quickly realized that the diversified island had advantages. Its commanding coast facing the sea offered an excellent 'lookout' to watch for invaders, while the land provided an excellent 'watering hole' for tired men to recuperate. Even today, motoring along the winding lanes over the gently undulating countryside, gazing out across the mud-flats and saltings which have changed little since the Roman occupation, proves to be a refreshing experience. Indeed, it has been said that the south-facing shore with its picturesque gardens has an almost Mediterranean feel about it.

The importance the Romans attached to Mersea during their occupation is not hard to discover. The base of a structure thought to be a Roman lighthouse stands at Pharos (which means lighthouse) Lane not far from West Mersea Church, and the 'Mersea Stone' at the south-east corner of the island was formerly the blockhouse of a military outpost.

Immediately opposite the island across the Blackwater Estuary at Bradwell is the site of the Roman coastal fort of Othona, still visible from Mersea today as it must have been in the first century. Now, however, the Bradwell nuclear power station close to this site overshadows everything else. It seems highly probable that Mersea was a staging-post through which Colchester sent supplies to maintain Othona. The significance of this proximity will feature again in our story.

Archaeological digs on Mersea have uncovered the remains of a number of impressive villas with tessellated pavements which were obviously the dwellings of officers living on the island. This also tends to support the theory that the Romans considered Mersea to be one of the healthiest spots in England, and sent their wounded and battle-weary men there to rest. There was also, of course, a garrison of troops on the island, ready to put to sea at any sign of the Vikings and their periodic raids on the east coast.

In time, of course, the Danes superseded the Romans and drew their longships up onto Mersea beach. It is said that Alfred the Great besieged a party of them on the island in AD 895. Blood was spilled again during the reign of Charles I when a small fort at East Mersea was occupied by the royalists until a party of Roundheads were detached from the siege of Colchester and sent to mop up the King's men and take possession of their ships. A few years later, according to the historian Thomas Cox, the island began to develop a settled population, 'and is now a place of great Strength and may almost be kept against the whole world; for which reason the Parliament put 1,000 men to guard from any attempt of the Dutch in the Dutch wars.'

Today, visitors come to Mersea to escape the clamour of modern life and enjoy its scenery, fine yachting facilities and beach resorts. Those epicureans in the know also come for the island's famous oysters, called 'West Mersea Natives', which can be bought on the seashore close to the old oyster storage pools – some of which are still in use. The 'Natives' are a delight to the palate, and even worth being cut off from the mainland to savour – as happened to some friends and I when we drove out one spring day for a little feast and forgot to check the time of the high tide!

As we waited on the island for the Strood to reappear from under the receding grey-green waters, we could make out on the other side the low huddled shape of an old inn, the Peldon Rose, where much of the history of the ghost of the Roman centurion has been collected and discussed over recent years.

The Peldon Rose is itself at least 400 years old, its ancient tiled roof surmounted by two massive chimneys and the low walls swathed in masses of beautiful climbing roses. Years ago, it is said, smugglers, men-of-war sailors, privateersmen and the odd pirate used it as a rendezvous, but now fishermen and farm labourer rub shoulders with tourists and residents of Colchester who have driven out for a pint or two of the inn's excellent ales.

It was one particular Victorian visitor to the pub, the Reverend Sabine Baring-Gould, who first committed to paper what until then had only been oral tales of the ghostly Roman soldier. Baring-Gould, who was the rector of East Mersea for several years in the 1880's, was a fascinating if somewhat eccentric character who mixed the life of a clergyman with that of a writer of esoteric fact and popular fiction. In fact, he published well over a hundred books on subjects as varied as theology, geography and folklore. He was also a composer and is perhaps best known of all for having written that stirring hymn, 'Onward Christian Soldiers'.

It was actually while he was living on the island that Baring-Gould became interested in the supernatural, an interest that was no doubt prompted by the stories he was told of local hauntings. He also heard the tale of a local beauty who had been kept a virtual prisoner by her drunken mother on Ray Island – a lonely strip of saltings on the edge of Mersea – and he turned this into a hugely successful Victorian melodrama, *Mahalah*. This made his name and later enabled him to retire to Devon and there devote the remainder of his life to writing.

Among Baring-Gould's still highly regarded (though now extremely rare) supernatural volumes are *The Book of Were-Wolves* which he published in 1865, and *A Book of Ghosts* which appeared in 1904. In this later work is to be found the first mention in print of the ghostly Roman centurion of Mersea Island.

According to Baring-Gould, local people claimed that for many years there had been reports of the figure of a Roman soldier patrolling the Strood at certain times of the year – especially on the night of the autumn equinox (around September 23). Several of these folk maintained that occasionally other figures had been seen approaching the man and the sound of the clash of swords had echoed across the mud-flats.

One particular version of this haunting intrigued Baring-Gould for it suggested that the men were not fighting the lone soldier, but actually helping him to repel invaders. Other tales of invisible feet heard marching across the causeway were similarly brought to the attention of the author-clergyman by the customers of the Peldon Rose.

Baring-Gould himself strolled across the Strood many times in the hope of seeing or hearing this phenomenon, but all to no avail. This did not, however, shake his belief in the authenticity of the legend.

'I believe the sounds the people of Mersea heard were the ring of the swords and the clang of the armour of Roman soldiery who fought and died here centuries ago. Whether there be one soldier or more I do not profess to know,' he concluded.

Sadly, Baring-Gould died before a particularly vivid testimony of an encounter with the ghost was provided by the landlady of the Peldon Rose in 1926. Her name was Jane Pullen and she was a woman whose integrity and force of character brooked no argument. Her story, in fact, confirmed the legend of the phantom centurion once and for all.

Mrs Pullen was a small, neat lady dressed invariably in black satin who possessed a commanding manner and a withering look. She continued to run the pub until well into her eighties and made the establishment a model of its kind. She believed in ghosts – she explained with quiet simplicity – because one night she had walked home with one from the Barrow Hill, a 20 ft high mound on the island, down to the Strood.

It was a warm, moonlit summer evening when Jane Pullen had her encounter with the supernatural as she was returning to the Peldon Rose after visiting some friends on the island.

'He came down off the mound at Barrow Hill,' she told enquirers later, in her matter-of-fact way. 'I heard the steady tramp of a man's feet – like he was a soldier marching. And he caught up with me as I was walking and walked with me all the way down to the Strood.

Though I looked about, I could see no-one – yet the sound of the feet were close beside me. So near I could have touched him.

'Several times I stopped to look along the road in the moonlight, but no-one was there. Still those feet kept on beside me.'

Mrs Pullen had nearly reached her destination when another extraordinary thing happened.

'I was walking down the causeway when I came upon a man I knew, one of the men who came to the Rose,' she went on. 'He was all a-tremble. He was shaking like a leaf. He said to me, "I can hear someone walking, but where is he? I can't see anyone."

'He could obviously hear the same as me. "Keep along of me," I said to the man, "and no harm will come to you. 'Tis only one of those old Romans come out of the Barrows to take his walk." And we walked on – with the footsteps close beside us – until we turned up the lane to the inn, at which the sound went on.'

The landlady's terrified companion was only too glad to take a steadying drink in the Peldon Rose as Jane Pullen recounted what they had both heard to a group of regulars in the bar. Without exception the men all knew better than to scoff at her story – indeed, most were already familiar with the legend of the ghostly soldier.

When, finally, one of the group asked Mrs Pullen if she had been frightened he received a withering glance and a terse reply. 'Why should I be?' the old lady asked. 'I put my trust in God – and, besides, those old Romans mean you no harm.'

The 'old Romans' – or one Roman in particular – caused no harm, either, to another Mersea resident who also found himself being accompanied on a walk across the Strood just before the outbreak of World War Two. This time, though, the man and his phantom companion were walking in the opposite direction to that taken by Jane Pullen – back *towards* the Barrow Hill.

Then again in 1956 two campers on Ray Island were disturbed in the middle of the night by the sound of unusual footsteps outside their tent. There was also a noise very reminiscent of armour clinking. Mystified, the couple plucked up courage and peered nervously out of the tent to find ... nothing. Nothing, that is, except the diminishing sound of what they subsequently became convinced had been the phantom centurion.

Some six years after this a remarkable event occurred at Barrow Hill Farm, a rather bleak-looking, brick-built farmhouse on which the Barrow Hill stands – and heightened the mystery still further. The farmhouse had for years been said to be haunted by ghostly knockings in the walls: but what happened then was even stranger.

A man – never subsequently named – was apparently digging on the mound when he suddenly felt the ground beneath him collapse and he fell into what seemed like a small cavern. When he had recovered and his eyes had adjusted to the gloom, the intruder found himself in a hollowed out chamber which bore all the signs of being a burial place. Without touching anything, the man clambered from what could so easily have become his own tomb and reported his discovery to the local authorities.

Later excavation in the mound brought to light a handful of Roman artifacts, including a funeral urn and some human ashes, and these seemed to confirm the belief that a Roman of some rank must have been buried there. Could it have been the man whose ghostly shade now walked the causeway that he had once patrolled in life?

Interestingly, this discovery seemed to rule out another quite different explanation for the phenomena of Barrow Hill which had been offered by a local historian Archie Wright in his book *Tideways and Byways in Essex and Suffolk* published in 1948. For Mr Wright believed that a Danish love triangle had been the cause of the ghostly sightings on Barrow Hill. He had written:

The Danes on Mersea not only had to contend with the Saxons, but fought among themselves. Two brothers fell in love with the same fair maiden. Who the lucky man should be could only be decided by force of arms. With their harness heavy upon them they fought hard and long throughout the day until, in the cool of the evening, and spent with exertion, they fell dead side by side. The maiden, stricken with grief, could no longer support life, and the trio were buried on Barrow Hill. Those of good hearing say that when the harvest moon rises in the fullness of her glory they hear the clash of sword and the clang of shield to shield. The night air is disturbed by harsh cries and hard breathing. The earth trembles a little as heavy bodies strike the ground. The old ones are at it again. There is the heartbreaking wail of the lady. As the moon wanes so does the tumult die. The brothers hack at each other with decreasing fury, the wailing sinks to a whimper, becomes a sob, and then all is quiet again. But I have never heard those things.

Those who *have* support the Roman explanation.

Following the intrusion into the grave in 1962 and the removal of the artifacts there was a feeling among local people that the phantom might never be seen again. But such a fear proved unfounded, for in February 1970 the ghost made another appearance – perhaps the most dramatic of all.

It was a cold winter's night, but the sky was clear and the island was free of mist. Two men, both members of the Royal Navy, were driving in a car over the Strood towards Mersea when something suddenly loomed up ahead in the vehicle's headlights. To their startled eyes it seemed like a human figure wearing a helmet, standing bolt upright, with vertical and horizontal white lines across it.

The driver attempted to brake as the figure rapidly filled his windscreen, and the car's tyres screeched agonizingly on the causeway. A flurry of startled birds flew up from the saltings as the car lurched to a halt in the middle of the road.

The two shaken occupants turned to look at one another. Had their senses deceived them? They had certainly run into *something* that looked like a man on the road – but there had been no sound, no ominous thump of a body being hit. They stepped uncertainly out of their vehicle to investigate.

All around was silence except for the fluttering of the

startled birds as they flew away across the dark expanse of Pyefleet Channel. There was nothing illuminated up ahead by the car's headlamps, nor was there any sign of a body underneath the vehicle or lying behind in the road. Both men were forced to agree that whatever they had struck had had no substance whatsoever.

The pair were rational and seasoned naval officers, trained in observing the sea in all its moods by day and night – but neither had ever seen anything quite like the phenomenon that had unfolded before them. And neither was aware of the legend of the ghostly centurion until they reported their experience later that night and were told all about the island's famous haunting.

Today, the two officers are convinced that it was the Roman soldier they ran through. They believe that the strange white lines they saw were the metal skirt of the man's tunic. The pair have actually been back to repeat their drive across the causeway on at least two subsequent February nights, but the ghost has not reappeared. For them at least.

Jill Keene who lives on Mersea and reports local events for the *Colchester Evening Gazette* has also become fascinated by the legend of the ghost of the Strood.

'Over the years, many people have claimed to have seen ghosts on the island,' she says, 'and in recent years we've had ghost hunters turning up on the night of the autumn equinox to try and see or hear something.'

Jill claims that recently the story has taken on a new element. Now apart from the centurion, the noise of what sounds like a Roman chariot has also been reported.

'Several people on the island say they have heard the sound of horses' hooves and cartwheels around autumn time on Mersea Island and Ray Island. Each of these stories seem uncanny in their resemblance to each other. The most convincing was told by a woman driving home to East Mersea who was convinced that she saw a chariot and horses cross the road in front of her near the Roman grave on Barrow Hill.'

What has caught the interest of a number of local experts in the supernatural about this story is its similarity to another phantom reported from the site of the old Roman fort of Othona on the opposite of the estuary near Bradwell. James Wentworth Day, who investigated this phantom, wrote a few years ago:

> There is a galloping ghost – the thunderous hoof-beats of an invisible man on an invisible horse – riding from the direction of Weymarks Beach on the south shore of the Blackwater Estuary, bang opposite Mersea Island. In short, the direct line of approach for a horseman from the Roman look-out tower on Mersea to the shore-castle of Othona. What more likely than it is a ghostly Roman Light Cavalryman going hell-for-leather to warn the garrison of Othona of an invading fleet sailing over the rim of the sea?

The most recent sighting of this phantom horseman was made in 1976 by a camper pitched close to the ancient chapel of St Peters-on-the-Wall, which was built on the actual site of the Roman fort in AD 654. The man was standing in the entrance of his tent, smoking a cigarette under the night sky, when he heard the sound of hoof-beats on the turf. In a statement made later, the camper – who wished to remain anonymous – said:

> My immediate reaction was that this was a ridiculous time of night to go riding, unless it was a stampeding cow. I made my way out of the tent, but my attention was drawn towards the sea-wall from whence the sound seemed to originate. However, I saw nothing, but couldn't help but feel rather mystified and tried to rouse my companion, who merely turned over and went back to sleep. I must emphasize that I had not then heard of the horse legend. Needless to say, some of my other companions put me right about what I must have heard. The local version of the haunting is that the centurion is riding from the direction of the estuary towards the site of the old Roman fort at Othona.

But to return to Mersea once again. In September 1989 there was a great flurry of excitement on the island when what at first appeared to be the best sighting of the centurion on the Strood for many years was reported. Sadly, it turned out to be a hoax, as Jill Keene later reported in the *Evening Gazette*.

'This elaborate hoax had numerous people sure that the centurion was on the move again,' she wrote. 'The hoaxers had cars positioned at each end of the Strood with car phones linking the two.

'Each time a car was reported to be turning back to get a second look at the "ghost", the man dressed in full Roman costume was quickly taken a little offshore in a dinghy until the coast was clear.'

Despite this prank, a number of ghost hunters have continued to keep an annual vigil on the road to Mersea. They were out again on the Strood during the night of the September equinox of 1991 as I was completing this book – and although aided by a glowing full moon and a high tide neither the centurion nor his chariot were witnessed.

But nevertheless the legend lives on discussed as earnestly as ever in the Peldon Rose and among the people of Mersea. A story of such longevity is unlikely to be ruined by the hoax perpetrated by those technological jokers – especially not on a coast as beset by mystery as that of East Anglia...

# 10   The Wizards of Canewdon

The stretch of bleak Essex coastline between Maldon and Southend, which includes the desolate areas known as the Dengie Marshes and Foulness Island, is often referred to in local conversation as 'The Witch Country'. Such an idea, with its visions of old crones riding on broomsticks, may well strike any listener as being rather odd: for the locality is no real distance from the Thames, and it is here, too, that there has been much debate about locating another airport for London.

It is soon evident, however, that old occult powers which modern science should have long ago dispoved are still referred to with respect by local people, while those who practiced them are mentioned with hushed admiration. The centre of these powers – according to those who have lived for generations on the triangular-shaped peninsular divided by the River Crouch – is the mysterious little village of Canewdon.

Although Canewdon can be reached comparatively easily by minor roads from the towns of Rochford to the north or Hockley to the west, it is not hard to imagine how remote it must have been during past centuries because of its situation amidst the Essex marshlands. Indeed, more than one writer referring to the names of the scattering of villages in the same locality – Ballards Gore and Snoreham are two that spring easily to mind – have declared that they 'sound like a route to the Middle Ages'. And true to this suggestion, the very name Canewdon, which means 'Hill of Cana's people', commemorates the fact that Canute landed here with his Danish army and went on to fight and defeat the Saxons at the Battle of Ashingdon.

The village itself, straddled along a single street, is dominated by the church of St Nicholas, the tower of which is believed to have been built on the orders of Henry V, to commemorate the great English victory over the French at the Battle of Agincourt in 1415. From the top of this 75 ft-high edifice – which was once used as a beacon for ships at sea and requires a climb of a hundred winding stairs to reach the top – it is possible to see a hundred square miles of Essex. The locals indeed claim that a visitor can see 'seven hundred churches' from the tower – but what they actually mean is that it is possible to see seven churches in the neighbouring 'seven Hundreds'. (It was Alfred the Great, of course, who originally divided the country into areas called 'Hundreds' and each of these into 'tithings', which we today refer to as parishes.)

Such prosaic facts, however, are soon forgotten when the visitor begins to discover the reason why the area is known as 'The Witch Country' and hears stories about the 'devil's masters'. These lived in Canewdon and practised their secret arts among the folk living in scattered marshland houses and little creek-side villages.

A clue to the reasons for the sinister reputation of Canewdon may first be gained by looking at the remnants of the 'cage' where malefactors were once locked up and the pond where, it is said, witches were once ducked. A resident, in fact, pointed out to me a field by the riverside known as 'The Witch's Field' because a witch was supposed to have been drowned in the river and buried there. For years it was believed that no crop would ever grow successfully there, she said.

It is in the oral traditions, however, that the facts about Canewdon become stranger still. One of the most enduring tales speaks of the devil's constant pursuit of the village's priest, who always managed to elude him by running along the narrow country lanes and causing the evil one to catch his tail in the hedgerows.

The church itself is also the subject of another legend. According to this, as long as the great tower remains standing there will be seven witches in the village – six females and 'the devil's master' who is always a man. But every time a stone falls from this edifice, one of the seven will die – though he or she will be immediately replaced. The tradition is even more specific about who these witches shall be: one will be the wife of the parson, a second that of the baker and the third the butcher's wife. Of the group as a whole 'there will be as many in silk as cotton', which is believed to be a reference to their social standing in the community. (As a matter of interest, at the time I was researching this story, the vicar was unmarried and there was neither a butcher nor a baker in the village.)

The most graphic account of one of these groups of Canewdon witches is contained in a report prepared by a local folklore expert, Eric Maple, which he based on interviews carried out among villagers in the late fifties. Although the report gives no clue as to the identity of the 'devil's master', the witches in question must have been alive in the closing years of the last century, Mr Maple claims.

> They were described as follows. Mrs W was a cripple who cast spells and was loathed for her venomous temper. Mrs K used to fix passers-by with her glaring eyes and prevented them from entering church. Mrs L was an eccentric who inflicted plagues of lice upon those who offended her.
>
> Another Mrs L betrayed herself as a witch by refusing to step over a doormat under which a steel knife had been laid. Mrs C was a woman renowned for bewitching waggonwheels and was known to possess imps. Mrs M was a not unkind woman, but one who occasionally terrified her neighbours by materialising spectrally at their bedsides in the dead of night, peering fiercely from beneath a poke bonnet.
>
> The activities of these sinister women were embodied in a wealth of macabre legend, no doubt passed down the generations for centuries and attached to one bevy of suspects after another.

The present day residents of Canewdon are, of course, well aware of the reputation of their village, but have, nevertheless, developed a rather engaging if macabre sense of humour about it.

According to one recent visitor to the parish, he overheard an old villager commenting on the arrival of a baby which had been born with a full set of teeth. 'My God!' the man exclaimed, 'the next thing we'll have here is werewolves!'

The Canewdon residents know that their predecessors lived for centuries in a locality which was both geographically and socially isolated, and all these people, most of whom were simple fishermen or farm labourers, had a deep-seated belief in the powers of the supernatural. Yet even today there is evidence of the continuing influence of the dark powers – in particular from something which recently occurred on the night of Hallowe'en (October 31).

Hallowe'en is, of course, the night when tradition says that the spirits of the dead can rise up from their graves for a last gambol before winter sets in. But while the nation's adults may have masked parties to remember and children everywhere recall the thrills of 'trick or treat', in Canewdon they talk instead of 'The Night of the Doll of Death' when they were given yet another reminder of the powers of the supernatural in their midst.

On the evening of 31 October 1976, some families living near the old wood known as The Scrub were suddenly roused from sleep by the sound of bloodcurdling screams and, from their window, saw among the trees a number of weird, flickering lights. Though no-one was brave – or foolish – enough to go to the woods that night, the following morning a 20 ft circle of logs covered with a mysterious white powder and a five-pointed pentacle were found in a clearing. At the centre of this lay a 12 inch long effigy of a naked woman, spiked to a log through her stomach and with six pins driven into vital parts of her anatomy.

This grotesque doll was also covered in blood-red candle grease and beside it stood a guttered black candle. What, though, most horrified the villagers who found it were the scores of footprints and hoofprints all around the clearing. No-one was in any doubt that the devil's work had been done there during the night, and a local expert on witchcraft who was called to the scene declared that the ritual had been performed to put a death curse on some unsuspecting victim in the vicinity.

Other evidence was subsequently collected on the peninsular. A sheep's heart pierced with thorns was found on a tombstone at Leigh-on-Sea. A bunch of weeping-willow leaves symbolising misery were placed in a newly dug grave at Rochford, and then followed by a serious motoring accident for the man who made the discovery – both incidents which convinced some of the older people of Canewdon that a 'devil's master' might well be active again. A man perhaps possessed of the same powers as the famous 'Cunning' Murrell who had lorded it over Canewdon in the Victorian era, or his successor the mysterious George Pickingale who worked the same ancient magic until just before World War One.

While nothing is, as yet, definitely known of a new 'devil's master', the facts about Murrell and Pickingale can be gleaned from records and local memories to provide a fascinating picture of arcane lore at work. And from these stories emerge portraits of men who were probably more like wizards than devil worshippers, though they undoubtedly exploited to the full the superstitious nature of the local population.

The man who came to be known as 'Cunning' Murrell, was born James Murrell in nearby Rochford in 1780. His was a long-established family and some of his descendants still live in the area today. That he was destined for a career as a 'witch doctor' seems to have been almost inevitable – for he was the seventh son of a seventh son.

After a brief period working for a shoemaker and a chemist (where he doubtless picked up a basic knowledge of medicine), James Murrell set himself up as a 'cunning man', claiming to have the power to exorcize evil spirits, heal humans and animals, restore lost or stolen property and read the future. Most particularly, he claimed to be able to cast out devils and neutralize the power of witches – all of these services were provided, of course, for a price.

Although no picture or photograph of Murrell has survived, he is described as having been a small man with a ruddy complexion. He dressed in a frock coat and wore a pair of iron-framed goggles which gave him a rather sinister appearance – especially to children. A Victorian author, Arthur Morrison, was the first person to visit Canewdon and write about Murrell – in an article called 'A Wizard of Yesterday' which was published in the *Strand Magazine* in 1900:

> From the tales I heard there never was such a mighty magician before, out of the Arabian Nights Entertainments. He was said to be miraculously transported from place to place in the night. He made a wonderful glass wherewith a man might see through a brick wall; he could do anything, cure anything, and know anything, past, present, or future, and it was his daily boast that he was the Devil's master'. In short, he was a white man-witch, and his powers many living men and women still testified to through all Essex...
>
> They told me of his marvellous cures, his amazing recovery of linen stolen from hedges, his surprising prophecies by aid of the stars, and his triumphant overthrowal of the wicked designs of witches. For Cunning Murrell, they would have me know, was a wizard who warred against the powers of darkness with all his might and it was no sin to employ the arts of a man like him. They told me, moreover, of the famous case of Sarah Mott, a young woman so devil-possessed and afflicted by witchcraft that she ran round tables without being able to stop, and walked about on the ceiling head downwards, like a bluebottle, till Cunning Murrell destroyed the witch's power over her and drove out the demon that possessed her.

Not everyone in the district shared these views about Murrell, however. There were dark rumours that he was also involved in smuggling on the Essex marshes and that it suited his ends to promote rumours of witches to keep people safely out of his way, tucked up in their beds. Other stories – not told in his hearing, one can be sure – maintained that he was actually in cahoots with some of the witches so that after they had put curses on selected victims he would conveniently arrive on the scene to remove them!

There seems little doubt that some of the incantations, which involved the blood of animals and the ground remains of insects, were more diabolical than any black magician might have conceived. Yet Murrell well deserved his sobriquet of 'Cunning': as a story related to me about him by an old resident of Canewdon makes abundantly clear.

It seems that on one occasion the wizard was trying to establish the identity of a thief, and made all the suspects pass through a darkened room in which a cock had been hidden under an earthenware pot. He asked each person to touch the vessel and claimed that the bird would crow when the thief touched it. Unbeknown to any of these people, he had earlier smeared the pot with a mixture of oil and blacking.

After all the suspects had passed through the room, my informant told me, and the cock had not made a sound, Murrell demanded to see their hands. Only one man had clean fingers. The cock had not crowed because the thief had not dared to touch the vessel, the wizard announced triumphantly!

Certainly 'Cunning' Murrell cultivated an atmosphere of mystery about himself, always keeping apart from community life. His cottage – now long since disappeared – was generally considered a place to avoid, especially at night when strange glowing lights were seen illuminating the tiny windows. This man, who greeted any timid knock at his door with a demand to know who was there and what they wanted, thunderously retorting that 'I am the devil's master!' was not someone to be trifled with or disturbed without a very good reason.

During his visit to the Essex marshes, Arthur Morrison also saw the trunk full of letters, papers and dusty old volumes which had been an integral part of 'Cunning' Murrell's trade, bequeathed to his son on his death. (This trunk and some of its contents, incidentally, are now on display at Southend in the Prittlewell Priory Museum.)

Morrison wrote afterwards:

> When I plunged into that dusty old box there came before
> my eyes heaps of letters and papers – all the sorrow and
> sickness and bedevillment of Essex, not to mention much
> of Kent and even some in London. There were many books
> of astrology, astronomy and tables of ascensions; many old
> medical books and botanical and anatomical plates, upon
> all of which Murrell had made a large number of additions
> and alterations to suit his purposes.

The author's words are doubly interesting in the clue they
provide to 'Cunning' Murrell's influence extending far
beyond the isolated Essex backwater in which he lived.
Morrison also wrote in his essay that the wizard claimed
to have the power to raise spirits – charging anything from
sixpence to half a crown for the service – though there
was aparently always some dispute in the community as
to whether these spirits were angels, as he said, or fiends
from hell as many others whispered.

Murrell was perhaps, though, most famous for his witch
bottles, curious iron receptacles he invented, made for him
by a local blacksmith. Into these he would put specimens
of the blood, nail pairings and strands of hair of any client
who suspected they were being cursed by a witch. The old
man then heated up the bottles in order to work 'counter
magic' whereby a burning sensation would be caused to
the body of the witch and force her to remove the spell.
According to another of my informants in Canewdon,
there were a number of instances where old women
suspected of spell-making were discovered with burns on
their bodies after Murrell had heated his bottles. In one
well remembered case a suspect had actually died when
one of the bottles overheated and exploded!

Cunning Murrell's reputation as a fortune-teller was
also widely known in southern England and it is said that
he predicted his own death 'to the very hour and minute'
– though there is no exact information as to when this was
beyond the date of 16 December 1860. The story, though,
just added to his legend; as did a claim by a rival wizard in

Raleigh that he had 'done for' Murrell with one of his own witch bottles – a claim laughed to scorn in Canewdon.

Though Murrell's body was subsequenly interred in an unmarked grave in nearby Hadleigh, his soul is said to have been unable to rest easy, and there are people in the Rochford Hundreds who claim that his ghost has returned time and time again as a reminder of the power he exercised.

Undoubtedly, the occult powers of this 'devil's master' were held in the highest regard by local people throughout his lifetime, and his name is still mentioned today with some awe. In truth, he contributed as much, if not more, to keeping alive Canewdon's occult traditions than his successor, George Pickingale.

In the case of this latter wizard, a photograph does exist which shows him to have been a tall, rather stooped figure, of unkempt appearance, with long fingernails and deep set, intensive eyes. He was ostensibly a farm labourer, lived in a little cottage near the Anchor Inn, and was known far and wide as a 'cunning man'.

Pickingale's great years of fame followed after the death of Murrell, and he is said to have augmented his hold on people through the power of his eyes. Indeed, it was believed his 'evil eye' could bring illness upon the animals of any neighbour who offended him and had the power to stop farm machinery. Pickingale boasted about his use of black magic and claimed to be descended from a long line of Canewdon witches. Rumours even said that he was able to call the local witches to his aid merely by blowing a wooden whistle.

Like 'Cunning' Murrell, he too courted notoriety, and his home was avoided because of the many tiny, staring red eyes which could be seen at his windows after nightfall. To some these were the pet mice he was known to keep, to others they were the imps he summoned up from who-knew-where to do his bidding.

Another legend maintains that Pickingale possessed the secret of flight and would ride on a hurdle at great speeds across the marshes. Certainly, he lived to the grand old age of ninety-three, dying in 1909 with a final flourish of his powers. For before his death and burial in the graveyard of St Nicholas's Church, he promised to show the local people that the power of the 'devil's master' would not pass with him. And as the hearse carrying his coffin arrived at the churchyard, the horses drawing it suddenly stepped from the shafts and galloped away.

Visitors to Canewdon today can be shown where Pickingale was buried in the old part of the churchyard, and also where his cottage stood until it finally collapsed in decay because no-one felt brave enough to live there. Another local story says that one of the wizard's two sons inherited his mantle, but this has not been substantiated and the man himself denied he was the 'devil's master' like his father.

A local historian Kathleen Cotton is, however, in no doubt that the wichcraft tradition lives on in Canewdon. 'You only have to go there on certain nights and you'll see the present seven witches holding forth on the banks of the River Crouch,' she says. And Ken Oliver, the landlord of the Plough and Sail Inn in the adjoining village of Paglesham has a better reason than most to believe the grip of the supernatural is as firm as ever on this part of the coast – for he has seen what is referred to as the 'Canewdon Ghost Witch'.

According to the story behind this haunting, years ago a middle-aged woman was condemned as a witch and executed. Shortly afterwards, villagers reported seeing her ghost materializing near the west gate of the churchyard, after which it would move down the hill towards the river. On other occasions the spectre was seen near the crossroads and close to where the ducking-stool had stood by the village pond. One man who came too close to the ghost said it had 'paralysing eyes' and as it passed him by, threw him to the ground with a 'mysterious force'.

Ken Oliver's encounter with this dangerous spirit occurred one night while he was driving home through Canewdon. 'Something black with staring eyes loomed up out of the darkness in front of my car,' he recalls with a shudder. 'There is only one way to describe what I saw ... it was a witch.'

No-one who visits Canewdon – especially by night – will, I am sure, choose to doubt Mr Oliver's statement. Electricity, television, and all the wonders of modern science may well be a part of most village homes now, but in the shadows the traditions of the past still linger on.

Until recently, for example, village children each year danced seven times around the church as a precaution against witchcraft, and there are still some old villagers who even today will not pass near the crossroads at night. For it is said that one of the devil's own was buried there years ago with a stake driven through her heart. My readers will not need reminding that this is the traditional way of ensuring that a vampire cannot leave its grave.

It may well be true that there is no practicing wizard in Canewdon, no 'devil's master' currently proclaiming his powers as Murrell and Pickengale did. But as one of my informants told me as I was leaving the village for the last time, that does not mean there is not one around somewhere on this witch-haunted landscape, so close to London and yet also so far away...